Touring Lower Manhattan

Three Walks in New York's Historic Downtown

Touring Lower Manhattan

Three Walks in New York's
Historic Downtown

Andrew S. Dolkart
and Steven Wheeler

New York Landmarks
Conservancy
2000

Design: The Oliphant Press, New York

Frontispiece: Lower Manhattan skyline from Brooklyn Heights, 1937

Contents

This publication was made possible by a grant from American Express Company.

Additional funding was provided by:
Furthermore, the publication program of
    The J.M. Kaplan Fund
The Bank of New York
The Witkoff Group
New York Stock Exchange
Skidmore, Owings & Merrill LLP
Sugar Foods Corporation
The Trump Organization

Foreword

New York City was born in Lower Manhattan. So were the co-sponsors of this book. American Express Company has been headquartered in Lower Manhattan since its start in 1850. The landmark American Express Company Building at 65 Broadway housed this burgeoning financial services firm from 1917-1975. The New York Landmarks Conservancy, created in 1973, focused first on saving endangered downtown landmarks such as the Fraunces Tavern Block and the U.S. Custom House. Since 1995, Heritage Trails New York, has literally put downtown on the map, guiding New Yorkers and legions of visitors alike to appreciate the rich history and diverse architecture of Lower Manhattan through its publications, tours, and markers.

Now, our three groups are proud to have commissioned a fresh look at this remarkable area, *Touring Lower Manhattan: Three Walks in New York's Historic Downtown*. We hope that you will enjoy this collaboration between architectural historian Andrew S. Dolkart, author of two other tourguides for the Conservancy, and Steven Wheeler, archivist of the New York Stock Exchange. We thank them for their fine work, a concise history of downtown architecture and commerce.

You are soon to read about, and hopefully to tour, Lower Manhattan. It is an extraordinary place! From a tiny Dutch toehold at the southern tip of Manhattan Island, the city grew rapidly northward, making the "downtown" distinction necessary. Here, economic titans forged the tools of American finance: banking, securities trading, capital markets, and the modern corporation. They built well and, often, very tall. In the historic core, under its canopy of great skyscrapers, and amidst the red brick buildings of nearby South Street Seaport, you may be surprised to discover a growing residential neighborhood as well. Also growing in Lower Manhattan is the inventory of designated landmarks and historic districts, ensuring that the protections of the City's Landmarks Law will preserve this historic and architectural legacy for future generations.

American Express, the Landmarks Conservancy, and Heritage Trails not only share a love for Lower Manhattan. We also believe that historic preservation enhances the quality of life in the downtown and encourages tourism in New York City. The great landmark buildings and districts in this book prove the point. We urge you to explore them with this guide in hand. We look forward to seeing you around the downtown — *Touring Lower Manhattan.*

Sincerely,

Harvey Golub, *Chairman & CEO*
American Express Company

Peg Breen, *President*
New York Landmarks Conservancy

Richard Kaplan, *Founder*
Heritage Trails New York

Acknowledgments

This walking tour was completed with the assistance of a great many people who generously gave their time and knowledge to the project. We would especially like to thank the librarians and archivists at the New York Public Library, New-York Historical Society, and Columbia University and the photographic curators at the New-York Historical Society and the Museum of the City of New York and the staff of the Corbis-Bettman Archives. At the Conservancy, we were grateful for the support of Peg Breen, President, and Roger Lang, as well as Ashley Williams Reick who undertook much of the photo research. Pioneering research has been undertaken on Lower Manhattan buildings by the research staff of the New York City Landmarks Preservation Commission and their designation reports were invaluable. Individuals who provided information or advice include Paris R. Baldacci, Mary Beth Betts, Susan Box, Norman Brouwer, Ken Cobb, Jonathan L. Coss, Jean Elliott, Christopher Gray, Gale Harris, Steve Johnson, Lauren Kaminsky, Jonathan Kuhn, Alexia Lalli, Daniel May, Christine G. McKay, Marjorie Pearson, Richard Pieper, Jay Shockley, and Carol Willis. Special thanks are due to our editor Susan Goldfarb and to Ron Gordon, Abe Brewster, and Andrew Sloat at Oliphant Press, the designers of this series of walking tour guides.

Introduction

The Architecture and Development of Lower Manhattan

Andrew S. Dolkart

Lower Manhattan is where New York City began, where the great commercial enterprises that fueled the city's growth were centered, and where, as *Architecture and Building Magazine* noted in 1920, "the worlds of shipping, finance and big business meet." No area of New York City has undergone more dramatic change than this compact section at the southern tip of Manhattan Island. The modest buildings of the 16th- and 17th-century colonial city rapidly gave way to wave after wave of commercial construction, culminating with the slender, soaring towers of the skyscrapers, erected in the late 1920s and early 1930s, that have come to define the Lower Manhattan skyline. The streets of Lower Manhattan are lined with some of New York's most famous buildings — Trinity Church, the New York Stock Exchange, and the World Trade Center. However, Lower Manhattan is also the site of extraordinary buildings that are not as well known but will thrill anyone interested in the city's architecture and history. The days when Dutch burghers, English gentlemen, Irish servants, African slaves and freedmen, and Yankee merchants roamed the narrow streets is long gone, yet one can still find physical traces from all of the layers of the area's past, if one knows where and how to look.

New York was initially colonized by the Dutch, who were interested primarily in exploiting the area's rich natural resources, especially in trading for furs with the Algonquin-speaking natives. The first European traders arrived in 1612, and two years later a colony was established. Almost from the start, the colony had a diverse

population: by 1643, a Roman Catholic missionary
reported that there were already people of eighteen
different nationalities living in the small settlement,
including Dutch, English, Irish, Scots, French, German,
Bohemian, Spanish, and Portuguese. Slavery had been
introduced in 1626 and New Amsterdam's African population increased rapidly — by 1703, people of African
descent accounted for 14 percent of the population.
The first Jewish immigrants settled in New Amsterdam
in 1654.

Unlike their counterparts in Philadelphia or Savan-
nah, the Dutch colonists made no effort to lay out a
planned community on Manhattan Island. The streets
of New Amsterdam ran in a haphazard manner, some

The 1660 Castello
Plan with the original
street pattern of New
Amsterdam: Broad-
way and Broad Street
are the wide thorough-
fares, with Greenwich
Street at left and Pearl
Street at right.

following topography or watercourses. One of the most extraordinary aspects of modern New York is the fact that the financial center of the nation is housed in massive office buildings that rise along the streets of colonial New Amsterdam. The Castello Plan, a map drawn in 1660, shows the city extending as far north as Wall Street (which did indeed have a wall). Most of the streets visible on this map are still extant, providing the only tangible remnant of the Dutch-colonial settlement.

In 1664, only four years after the Castello Plan was drawn, the British sailed into the harbor and Dutch governor Peter Stuyvesant surrendered the town to new colonial rulers. The English renamed the tiny settlement New York, but made few immediate substantial changes to its physical character. As the population grew, the density of development along the old streets increased. New streets were laid out to the north of the wall, and beginning in the late 17th century, new land was created by filling in the shoreline. Still, New York remained a compact place. In the 1760s, when Trinity Church decided to erect a chapel, it chose a site that was still farmland, located less than a mile north of the Battery. St. Paul's Chapel (NW1) is the one major survivor from the period when New York was an important colonial port. Its northern location saved St. Paul's from fires set during the Revolutionary War and from destruction by the Great Fire of 1835, which destroyed most of the city's oldest buildings.

Until the final years of the 18th century, New York was a city where people lived and worked in the same area, often in the same building. However, as the population grew (by 1800 New York had a population of more than 60,000, and by 1810 it was the largest city in North America), and as commerce rapidly expanded, people began to seek homes to the north, in newly developing residential neighborhoods. By the early 19th century, the Wall Street area and the East River waterfront were increasingly given over to business and commerce, with residential communities surviving to the south, near Bowling Green, and to the west of Broadway. The new commercial buildings, referred to at the time as counting-houses, had the modest scale of residential structures, but were planned exclusively for use by those involved in trade. This is most evident today in the South Street Seaport area, especially at Schermerhorn Row (NW21) on Fulton Street, erected in 1810-12.

It was during this period that Wall Street began to evolve into one of New York's most significant streets. Wall Street begins at Broadway, New York's major north-south thoroughfare, and extends only a few blocks to the East River. It is anchored at its western end by Trinity Church (WS1), the city's oldest Episcopal congregation. At Wall Street's junction with Broad and Nassau streets stood the first City Hall, site of the nation's first capital (1789 to 1790). It was on Wall Street that many of the city's wealthiest citizens lived in the late 18th century and where the city's first banks and insurance companies soon established their offices. In 1798 both the Bank of New York and the New York branch of the First Bank of the United States moved into elegant new buildings on Wall and William streets. These early commercial buildings had facades that closely resembled those of nearby residential buildings in both style and scale. Most companies seeking office

Wall Street and William Street in 1798 showing Bank of New York, Walton House (converted into New York Insurance Company) and the First Bank of the United States.

space did not erect new buildings, but converted old houses instead. For example, the Wall Street mansion located between the two bank buildings mentioned above was converted into the new home of the New York Insurance Company in 1800.

As wealth increased in New York and commercial and financial firms multiplied and expanded, the scale and sophistication of new buildings erected in Lower Manhattan increased as well. Individual businesses, speculative real estate developers, and government agencies commissioned impressive new structures, often faced in granite, marble, or other expensive stone. Many were designed by one of a growing roster of professional architects who were establishing offices in New York and turning the city into a leader in American architecture. Notable among the impressive new buildings erected on Wall Street during the 1820s and early 1830s were the Merchants' Exchange (Martin E. Thompson, 1824-27; demolished) and Phenix Bank (attributed to Martin E. Thompson, c. 1825-27; demolished), the city's first major Greek Revival building. Architect Ithiel Town introduced a new type of commercial architecture, based on the model of the New England warehouse, at his Tappan Store on Pearl Street of 1829 (demolished), a building with an austere granite facade and a ground floor of post-and-lintel construction. This building became the model for the counting-houses of the next decade, including the Hickson Field Store and other buildings in the South Street Seaport area (NW18 and NW22).

Ithiel Town's design for the Tappan Store, 1829.

Much of the old building fabric of Lower Manhattan — more than 700 structures — was destroyed in the Great Fire which burned for two days and nights in December 1835. The reconstruction that immediately followed heralded the stylistic prominence of the Greek Revival. New counting-houses modeled after the Tappan Store were erected near the waterfront, and impressive temple-fronted banks and office buildings appeared on or near Wall Street, proving the *New York Mirror* correct when it remarked in 1840 that "there is probably no business street in the world — certainly not in the

16

United States — that can exhibit so much architectural elegance. Wealth in Wall-street does not choose to dwell in humble mansions." Two of the greatest buildings of the era survive — the U.S. Custom House, now Federal Hall National Memorial (WS5) and the second Merchants' Exchange (WS12).

By the late 1840s, the Greek Revival that had been so popular for banks and commercial buildings in the 1830s had lost favor. As *Putnam's Magazine* noted in 1853, "In architecture as in history Greece has fallen victim to Italy." Instead of the columns and austere detail of Greek temples, the new commercial buildings of Lower Manhattan were modeled after the Renaissance palaces of Rome, Florence, and other Italian cities. The new buildings, with their marble or sandstone fronts, were generally four or five stories tall, with far more office space than earlier buildings. Most of the Italianate commercial palaces that rose on Wall Street, Pine Street, William Street, and other streets in the heart of the financial district were planned with easily adaptable space that could be rented to several different firms, making these some of the first speculative office buildings in the city. This was true even when the client was a major bank such as the Hanover Bank (the one example that survives; WS19) or the Manhattan Company. The bank might occupy space in the rear of the main floor, but the remainder of the building was rented to other banks, or to insurance companies, lawyers, brokers, and others involved in the business dealings of the day.

Despite the stylish grandeur of the facades of the new commercial buildings and the elegant appointments of the interior banking halls, these were not always ideal places in which to work. A report on sanitary conditions in New York City published in 1866 commented on the bleak conditions in many of the business structures of the financial district:

> Of the nearly two thousand buildings that are devoted to mercantile and business purposes in this district, only a small minority have adequate ventilation and lighting in their counting-rooms....We

know it is safe to say that hundreds and probably thousands of valuable lives are sacrificed every year in the counting-rooms, banking-houses, stores and offices of the commercial district of our city in consequence of defective ventilation and natural lighting; and that the health of a hundred thousand business men and their employés [sic] suffers seriously from the same causes.

By the outbreak of the Civil War in 1861, most of Lower Manhattan to the east of Broadway had been transformed into a bustling commercial district lined with warehouses, banks, and office buildings. The scale of these buildings remained modest, with the tower of Trinity Church still soaring above all other structures. Most sectors of New York's economy boomed during the war as the city's financiers backed the Union's war effort and provided loans to industries that turned out products for the war effort. Following the war, the wealth accumulated by New York's businesses was used to erect grander and more technologically advanced buildings, setting the stage for the innovative Lower Manhattan skyscrapers that would profoundly alter the nature of commercial architecture.

The building that set the stage for the development of the skyscraper was the Equitable Life Assurance Society's headquarters on the corner of Broadway and Cedar Street (1868-70; demolished), immediately across from Trinity Church's graveyard. Gilman & Kendall's design may have been traditional in its use of the French Second Empire style, but the eight-story structure was revolutionary in its incorporation of passenger elevators. The elevator altered the nature of the office building. For the first time, the upper stories of a commercial building were more valuable than floors closer to the street. Equitable occupied the less valuable lower floors, profiting from the substantial rents received from firms occupying the higher floors. Structurally, the Equitable and its immediate followers employed traditional masonry construction, augmented with cast-iron columns and wrought-iron beams.

Wall Street looking west from Pearl Street, c.1878.

Construction in New York City virtually ceased in 1873 as the result of a serious financial panic. When building began again in the 1880s, iron was employed more extensively in tall structures such as the Corbin Building (NW3), one of the few office buildings of this era to survive in Lower Manhattan. The 1888-89 construction of the narrow Tower Building (demolished; see p. 61), the earliest New York building with a steel skeleton frame, altered the nature of skyscraper design, almost immediately resulting in the construction of such monumental buildings as the Bowling Green Offices (BB12), the Empire Building (BB17c), the Trinity and U.S. Realty buildings (NW9a and 9b), the American Surety Building (NW10), and the enormous Equitable Life Assurance Building (NW11) that replaced the earlier building which had burned. Other technological

Equitable Life Assurance Company Building, after 1889. Original 1868-70 section at left, with 1886-89 addition.

innovations were also crucial, including new developments in wind bracing and, most significantly, in foundation construction. This was a necessity in an area where tidewater and quicksand are often not far beneath the surface.

The architects who designed the first generation of New York skyscrapers, ending in 1916, were not interested in developing a new architectural style for the new type of building. Rather, they adapted the traditional styles popular at the time to the demands of the tall building. Thus, there are Romanesque Revival skyscrapers such as the Wallace Building (NW13); Neo-Gothic skyscrapers such as the Trinity and U.S. Realty buildings (NW9a and b); buildings with Classical detail, such as the Bankers Trust (WS4) and American Telephone and Telegraph (NW2) buildings; and others, like the Empire Building (BB17c), displaying Renaissance detail.

Most of the skyscrapers in Lower Manhattan were constructed as speculative ventures by builders or syndicates of investors interested in maximizing their returns by erecting the largest structure that was economically feasible on a given site and leasing space to a large number of different tenants at the highest possible rents. The most prolific architect of these speculatively-built skyscrapers was the firm of Clinton & Russell which designed the Broad-Exchange Building (BB18) and many other late-19th- and early-20th-century skyscrapers. The firm was adept at laying out floors to maximize rental space, while at the same time offering tenants such amenities as elegant lobbies, efficient elevator service, modern plumbing and heating, and as much light and air as a site would allow. The buildings designed by Clinton & Russell and the other architects who specialized in speculative skyscrapers generally have limestone bases, imposing entrances, brick upper floors, and decorative terra-cotta detail.

Some of the most prominent skyscrapers were built by specific banks or corporations or by syndicates working with a specific business. Such buildings tend to have distinguished facades with especially elaborate ornamentation. Often these signature buildings were planned with unusual rooftop profiles that served to identify them and to advertise their corporate sponsors. Among these distinctive buildings were the Singer Building, with its narrow tower (demolished), which was, for a brief period, the world's tallest building, and the Bankers Trust Building (WS4), with its crowning stepped pyramid which not only was one of the most visible elements of the Lower Manhattan skyline for many years, but became the emblem of the bank.

Skyscrapers are associated in the public's mind with Wall Street and the other canyon-like streets of the Financial District. However, skyscrapers actually came quite late to Wall Street and the streets adjoining. This was partially due to the general conservatism of the bankers and brokers who ruled these streets, but the fact that Wall Street is a narrow thoroughfare with no open space that would guarantee light and air also inhibited investment in tall buildings for many years. In fact, the earliest skyscrapers clustered along lower Broadway and were especially evident on plots overlooking the open spaces of Bowling Green and Trinity Church's grave-yard. By 1912 Lower Broadway was lined with tall buildings, but, as the *Real Estate Record and Builders Guide* reported, Wall Street was "a thoroughfare of compara-tively low buildings. Compared with lower Broadway, from Bowling Green to the City Hall, it has few tall structures. Its average of tall buildings is, indeed very low. Of the sixty-three structures on its entire length, nearly 50 percent, are five stories or less, only a dozen are twelve stories or more and only two are more than eighteen stories high."

The development of the skyscraper caused land values in Lower Manhattan to skyrocket, since property was now valued for its potential to support a tall build-ing. This did not, however, preclude certain owners from building structures of modest scale, even as sky-scrapers were rising on surrounding sites. As tall build-ings competed for light and air and for a prominent place on the skyline, wealth and power could be expressed by erecting a modestly-scaled building on a vastly expensive piece of land. The most conspicuous example of this trend was the building erected by J.P. Morgan as the headquarters for his bank (WS6). Not only was this modest structure erected on one of the most valuable sites in New York — the intersection of Wall and Broad streets — it actually replaced Morgan's previous headquarters structure which was taller. Lee, Higginson & Company (BB19), the American Bank

Note Company (BB22), the New York Stock Exchange (WS7), the U. S. government (for its Assay Office on Wall Street; WS8), and the Chamber of Commerce of the State of New York (NW31) also erected modestly-scaled buildings on prominent and expensive pieces of property, each organization proclaiming its importance with a building that was far smaller than what a speculative builder would have erected on the same plot of land.

The first generation of skyscraper construction ended with the appearance of several enormous buildings that rose straight up from their lot lines with no setbacks. The scale of buildings such as those on lower Broadway had generated a debate on the issue of regulating the construction of tall buildings. Some argued for strict regulations in order to guarantee that light would reach the streets and sidewalks. Others — notably the architect Francis Kimball, who was a leading skyscraper designer (see p.120) — strongly opposed any regulation. The city decided not to cap the height of buildings, but instead developed a regulation that would require setbacks. In 1916 New York City became the first municipality in the country to institute a zoning code (see p. 125). The law had little immediate impact because America's entry into World War I brought construction to a halt.

The massing of the skyscrapers erected during the building boom of the 1920s and early 1930s was totally different from that of earlier skyscrapers and profoundly changed the nature of the Lower Manhattan skyline. Stylistically, some of the buildings erected in the post-World War I period — notably the Standard Oil (BB11) and Cunard (BB14) buildings — had facades that were as conservative as those erected in earlier decades, however, many of the most spectacular buildings from this period — the Irving Trust Company (WS3) and Cities Service (NW15) buildings, to name just two examples — employ the Art Deco ornament that became popular in the last years of the 1920s. Architects of this period also created some of the greatest public interiors in New York. Buildings such as those occupied by Cunard, Irv-

ing Trust, and Cities Service have interiors ornamented with varicolored veined marbles, travertine, ornate plaster work, bronze, nickel-silver, and other materials, and their lobbies, banks, and ticket-booking halls are often embellished with murals and mosaics.

In the hands of a talented architect, the setbacks required by the new zoning law could be manipulated to create structures with dynamic massing that also maximized rentable space. Ely Jacques Kahn, Sloan & Robertson, and other architects created expressive buildings by manipulating the setback rules, as is evident on John Street (NW26), where Kahn and several other architects designed buildings for the insurance industry, and at Sloan & Robertson's 29 Broadway (BB15) and Maritime Exchange Building (BB24). The zoning code permitted towers to rise to any height that was economically feasible on 25 percent of a lot. This accounts for the form that is most closely associated with skyscrapers of this era — a massive base with setbacks, capped by a slender tower soaring into the sky. The four great towers from this era in Lower Manhattan — those of the Irving Trust Company (WS3), the Manhattan Company (WS9), City Bank-Farmers Trust (WS15), and Cities Service (NW15), came to define the romantic skyline of New York, famous to all those who sailed into New York's harbor. A symbol of the dynamism of New York,

Cities Service and Manhattan Company towers soar above the modest counting-houses of the old seaport city. Drawing by John C. Wenrich, 1935.

they became a readily identifiable image in countless Hollywood movies and the inspiration for many photographers. These great towers soared above the modest early-19th-century counting-houses that still stood along the waterfront, creating a dramatic contrast between the early trading city and the great business and financial center of the 20th century. The towers housed the offices of the companies for which they were named, but most of the floors were intended as income-producing rental space. These buildings and others were erected during a construction boom in the late 1920s and early 1930s, but the boom was cut off as the city began to feel the impact of the Crash of 1929 and the resultant Great Depression. It was ironic that as the heights of the buildings rose, the stock market plunged, radically reducing the need for office space as businesses failed or retrenched.

After World War II, New York's economy, along with that of the rest of the nation, entered a period of prosperity, but this prosperity was not shared by many of the building owners of Lower Manhattan. Following a trend that began in the 1920s, many of the corporate headquarters, banks, and law firms of Lower Manhattan moved to new offices in Midtown. Land values fell, and the vacancy rate in the aging office buildings of Lower Manhattan increased. Something dramatic needed to be done in order to stabilize the economy of Lower Manhattan. The 1955 announcement that the Chase Manhattan Bank, a major landowner in the area, would erect a gleaming Modern headquarters structure on a two-block site was just such an event. Gordon Bunshaft's aluminum and glass building (NW12) changed the character of office construction in Lower Manhattan. The building occupies only 30 percent of its site, rising on a plaza that was the first new open space created in densely-built up Lower Manhattan since the 18th century.

The success of the Chase Manhattan Building led to a construction boom in the 1960s, especially after the zoning law was rewritten in 1961 to promote the tower-and-plaza form first seen downtown at Chase.

Unfortunately, with rare exceptions — notably Gordon Bunshaft's Marine Midland Building (NW8) and I.M. Pei's Wall Street Plaza (NW16) — the new buildings were undistinguished. Many of them were constructed near the East River waterfront, replacing the early 19th-century counting-houses. The destruction of the old seaport buildings generated concern that the city's maritime history was about to disappear. The effort to save part of the old commercial district resulted in the establishment of the South Street Seaport Museum in 1967 and the beginning of the campaign to preserve and restore the surviving buildings from the first generation

Chase Manhattan Bank Building flanked by Manhattan Company and Cities Service buildings, 1978.

of New York's commercial architecture.

The economic downturn of the mid-1970s, coupled with the opening of the World Trade Center's twin towers (NW6) — which attracted many businesses previously housed in older Lower Manhattan buildings — caused the office market to collapse once again. As more and more office space was vacated, residential conversion of these buildings began. The adaptive reuse of the Cotton Exchange (WS16) and Liberty Tower (NW30) as apartment buildings added a residential component to the area that had been lacking since the early 19th century.

Since the 1970s, Lower Manhattan has gone through periods of boom and bust. In the early 1980s, several enormous new buildings were erected, including those housing Goldman Sachs (BB27), J.P. Morgan & Co. (WS13), and Prudential Securities (NW25). These massive structures have the huge floor areas that many companies demanded so that they can accommodate computers, conference rooms, and other uses that do not require windows. The design of these buildings also reflects the fact that air conditioning and fluorescent lighting has made natural light and air from operable windows unnecessary in modern office construction.

In the early 1990s many urban planners again feared that Lower Manhattan would lose its competitive edge as a new wave of corporations moved out of the area, relocating their administrative offices to Midtown and their back-office operations (computer facilities, payroll, etc.) in Brooklyn or the suburbs. The city instituted tax incentives for rehabilitating buildings in Lower Manhattan or for converting them into apartments. By the middle of the decade there had been a wave of residential conversions, including the transformation of the Empire (BB17c) and Broad-Exchange (BB18) buildings into luxury apartments. However, by the end of the millennium real estate values had again increased in Lower Manhattan, and several buildings, including the Manhattan Company (WS9) and the City Bank-Farmers Trust (WS15) were upgraded for continuing use as offices.

Lower Manhattan continues to be one of the most

diverse sections of New York. A visitor can walk along the granite streets of the early-19th-century seaport city and, only a few minutes later, explore the lobby of a great Art Deco office tower; one can stand in awe at the transparency of the Chase Manhattan Bank's Modern glass tower and then turn around and examine the dynamic masonry skyline of the early-20th-century towers rising on or near Wall Street. Walk along the colonial-era streets of Lower Manhattan, enter office-building lobbies, peer up at the decorative ornament on buildings large and small, and enjoy the richness of architecture and history nestled at the southern tip of Manhattan Island in New York's historic commercial center.

John Wenrich's c. 1929 rendering of the Irving Trust Company Building (WS3) rising above Trinity Church.

Lower Manhattan:
New York's Capital Center

Steven Wheeler

Lower Manhattan is one of the world's leading financial centers, home to international banks, stock and commodities exchanges, insurance companies, brokerage firms, and money managers. Wall Street is the historic core of the financial district and something of a symbol in itself. More than just a street name, Wall Street is recognized the world over as the business of money, a symbol of supreme financial power, and a label applied to the entire neighborhood of downtown skyscrapers and financial institutions.

Bird's-eye view of New York, c. 1850. Sailing ships and steamboats crowded the harbor and docks that lined the Lower Manhattan shore.

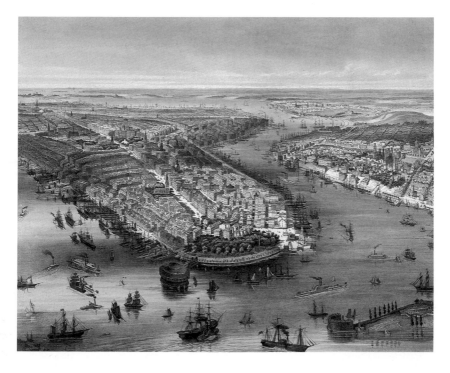

The financial district is also New York City's birth-place. Two centuries ago, New York City was still a modest settlement perched at the southern tip of Man-hattan Island. Wall Street, one of the town's most prominent thoroughfares, was the geographic middle of the city as well as the growing center of economic, political, and social life. A walk along Wall Street revealed a mix of public institutions, elegant town-houses, and commercial establishments, inhabited by a diverse population. At one end stood the city's most prestigious house of worship, Trinity Church. At the other end were the East River wharves and warehouses of shippers and merchants who moved goods into and out of the city. Between them was Federal Hall, home to two sessions of Congress and the site of Washington's inauguration as president. The Merchants' Coffee House and the Tontine Coffee House, noted more for political debate and commercial dealings than for coffee, were catercorner, at Wall and Water streets. The Bank of New York greeted its customers in an elegant new building at the corner of William Street, an indication of Wall Street's financial future. All along the street were homes of merchants, lawyers, artisans, and other citizens, the wealthier ones near Trinity Church and the more mod-est ones toward the river and docks.

Today New York City's midtown has shifted far uptown, its social elite resides in apartment houses along Park Avenue, and sightseers and commuters are the only things that land by boat in Lower Manhattan. Yet Wall Street is still the economic center of the city.

The banks, brokers and other financial companies that are concentrated in Lower Manhattan drive the city's economy, accounting for a total economic output of $75 billion in 1997. The 160,000 people who work in New York's financial district firms make up only 5 percent of the city's total labor force, yet they account for 56 percent of the city's recent growth in real earn-ings. Even more important, Wall Street orchestrates the flow of capital around the world. New York City is the recognized financial capital of the globe, and Wall Street is the worldwide symbol of high finance.

New York City's destiny as a financial capital was determined in part by its geography. Its sheltered, deep harbor and island location made it a natural for shipping, and its position at the mouth of the Hudson River offered easy access to resources and markets upstate. A 1796 issue of *The New-York Prices Current*, the city's first business newspaper, indicates the great variety of commodities that were landed at the East River docks: brazilwood, Albany pine, mahogany, nails, glass, coal, Carolina indigo, pig iron, beaver pelts, codfish, whale oil, cotton, sugar, tobacco, molasses, Spanish brandy, English cheese, Jamaican rum, Souchong tea, and a dozen kinds of wine. By 1810, New York City had surpassed Philadelphia and Boston as the largest American city and the nation's busiest port.

After the Erie Canal opened in 1825, connecting New York's port with the Great Lakes, the city's preeminence as the nation's major trader was clinched. Grain and flour from the agricultural Midwest could be shipped from Buffalo to New York in eight days and then on to foreign markets at a fraction of the previous cost. Robert Fulton's *Clermont*, launched in 1807, began steamship trade along the Hudson River between New York and Albany. Transatlantic steam-packet service followed in the 1830s. By the mid-19th century, with swift clipper ships carrying tea, silk and other precious cargoes from China, New York's port handled more goods and passenger traffic than those of all other U.S. cities combined.

The city's success as a port gave rise to a great class of merchants who quickly became familiar with economic risk. These importers, exporters, wholesalers, and traders forged relationships with merchants overseas and accumulated financial knowledge, capital, and wealth. Merchant trading occurred at the countinghouses, warehouses, taverns, and coffeehouses that lined Wall Street and the district near the South Street docks. Construction of the first Merchants' Exchange on Wall Street in 1827 provided a convenient place for merchants to transact business and gave Wall Street a lasting role as the center of mercantile trade.

The financial services that would become central to Lower Manhattan's economic success — banking, insurance, and securities trading — developed during the late 18th and early 19th centuries as a natural extension of the merchants' business. The first bank established in New York was the aptly named Bank of New York (WS11). Founded in 1784 by Alexander Hamilton, it settled in Wall Street in 1798 and is still a presence there. It was followed in 1791 by the federally chartered Bank of the United States, which set up shop two doors down

Banks issued their own paper money until the 1860s. This one dollar note depicts the Bank of New York's home at 48 Wall Street.

from the Bank of New York. In the city's developing economy, banks were important facilitators of trade. Besides accepting deposits from customers, they made loans to commercial endeavors, discounted notes, traded bills of exchange, and dealt in foreign currency. Until the federal government began printing greenbacks in the 1860s, chartered banks issued bank notes which were circulated as currency in business and trade.

As the city's commerce flourished, other banks naturally followed. By 1812 there were eight banks in New York City, all of them headquartered in Wall Street. Some were created as sidelines to a company's original manufacturing purpose: the Bank of the Manhattan Company began as a water company in 1799, and Chemical Bank (1824) as a manufacturer of medicines and dyes. New York banks developed correspondent relationships, accepting deposits and clearing bank notes and checks for regional banks upstate and in the Midwest. By 1830 New York was the commercial banking center of the country.

The insurance business also developed to support port activities. Until the 1790s, merchants and shippers usually bought marine insurance from Lloyd's of London. The first American insurance company, the Insurance Company of North America, was founded in Philadelphia in 1792, inspiring the creation of two New York marine insurers in 1794: the United States Insurance Company and the Pacific Insurance Company. Marine insurance protected against loss of a ship and its cargo as well as loss of prospective freight earnings. The risk was often spread among two or three insurers. It was a prosperous business, particularly during New York City's clipper-ship era. Fire insurance was offered by the New York Insurance Company (1798) and others, but because of poor capitalization, inadequate fiscal supervision and exposure to risk, fire insurance was an unstable line of business for many years. Of the city's 26 fire insurance companies in business in 1835, all but three were wiped out paying claims arising from the Great Fire of 1835 (see p. 99). The disaster compelled insurance companies to reduce their risk in a particular locality by selling portions of it to other insurers, a branch of insurance known as reinsurance.

Until the 1840s, life insurance was generally a short-term policy covering the life of a traveler during a hazardous journey, or a tontine agreement where the insured had to outlive other policyholders to collect. The New York Life Insurance and Trust Company began selling life insurance contracts in 1830, popularizing the concept, but modern life insurance took off when mutually owned companies made policies more affordable. The Mutual Life Insurance Company wrote its first life insurance policy in 1843 and developed the industry's first mortality table to scientifically evaluate risk and determine the size of premiums. The Equitable Life Assurance Society (NW11), founded in 1859 by a disgruntled Mutual Life employee, quickly grew into an industry leader by using a large, enterprising sales force and aggressive marketing strategies. By 1870, more than two hundred marine, fire, and life insurance company offices were located along lower Broadway, Wall Street, and adjacent blocks.

As in banking, Alexander Hamilton also had a hand in developing New York City's securities market, though in a less direct way. Then, as now, there were two basic types of securities that were traded: stocks and bonds. A bond, whether issued by a government or a corporation, was essentially a loan. The investor paid the face value of the bond (usually in denominations of $1,000) and received interest payments from the issuer over the course of a specified number of years. At the end of the term, the bond was redeemed and its face value repaid to the bondholder. A stock, on the other hand, was issued only by a corporation and represented a share in ownership of the enterprise. Profits earned by the corporation were distributed to stockholders through annual dividends and the value of a stock would fluctuate as the corporation's earnings grew or declined.

The New York Stock Exchange in 1853 with members' assigned chairs (the origin of the term "seat" connoting membership in the exchange).

As the first Secretary of the Treasury, Hamilton created a plan to pay off the nation's Revolutionary War debt by selling $80 million worth of bonds to the public. The plan was a great success: investors bought the bonds in droves, purchasing the entire issue outright. Merchants began trading the bonds as part of their normal course of business, along with bills of exchange, promissory notes, and other commercial paper. In 1792 a group of 24 merchants who were actively trading the government bonds gathered beneath a buttonwood tree on Wall Street and signed an agreement to trade with one another, forming the basis of the New York Stock Exchange (WS7). The stock market developed slowly because of the relatively small number of securities available for trading — three classes of federal bonds and the stocks of the Bank of the United States and Bank of New York — and because of the economic difficulties presented by the outbreak of the War of 1812.

After the war, the stock market was set on a firmer footing when the New York Stock & Exchange Board was formally established in 1817 (the name was shortened in 1863). Its constitution set down rules for the transaction of business and the admission of members, and it imposed fines to keep unruly brokers in check. The members met twice daily in a rented room at 40 Wall Street to trade a list of thirty securities: federal, state and city bonds and the stocks of local banks and insurance companies. In 1827 they moved to the newly completed Merchants' Exchange (WS12).

Originally, securities were sold directly to public investors by subscription, and the earliest issues of federal bonds and Bank of the United States stock easily found eager buyers. As the need for capital increased — to fund construction of roads, bridges, and canals, or to support a war — merchants stepped in as middlemen to help corporations and the government find buyers for their securities. This resulted in the development of a new line of business called investment banking. In 1813 the fur trader John Jacob Astor became one of New York's first investment bankers when he and two other merchants purchased from the U.S. government

$10 million in unsubscribed war bonds at a discount and resold them at a profit to investors.

Most capital investment in America during the 19th century came from Europe and was funneled though Wall Street investment banks. Top-shelf "Yankee firms" like Prime, Ward & King and J. P. Morgan & Company (WS6) depended on strong ties to European financial institutions and markets (Morgan's father was one of London's most powerful bankers, for instance). Another class of important investment banks was created by German Jews who had emigrated to America in the 1830s and 1840s. Active in mercantile trade, they drew on valuable connections to investors and capital back home and developed into powerful and durable investment banks. This group included Goldman Sachs (BB27), Lehman Brothers (WS17), and Kuhn Loeb & Company.

The Civil War created an extraordinary need to raise capital and helped the investment banking community mature. The Philadelphia bank Jay Cooke & Company developed the domestic retail market for Civil War bonds, selling $500 million to American investors. The firm employed a wide network of traveling agents and advertising that appealed to patriotic sentiment. J. & W. Seligman & Company (WS17), a firm of eight German-Jewish brothers, sold another $200 million in war bonds in the German market — a significant accomplishment, given the Union's damaged credit rating.

The favorite speculative securities by far during the 19th century were railroad stocks and bonds. In 1830 the first railroad stock was listed at the New York Stock Exchange — the Mohawk & Hudson Railroad, a line that carried 300 passengers a day between Albany and Schenectady. Railroads opened the West and drove the nation's economy, bringing producers closer to their markets, creating jobs, and spurring other industries such as steel. The railroads required more capital than other 19th-century endeavors, and by the end of the century, railroads were king of the stock market. More than 600 railroad stocks and bonds were listed at the New York Stock Exchange, and they accounted for the most actively traded securities.

Wall Street, looking east from Broad Street towards the Merchants' Exchange in 1864. The four- and five-story buildings housed offices of insurance companies, banks, stockbrokers, and lawyers.

Railroad finance also inspired spectacular battles between Wall Street's first celebrities, the "robber barons" of the Gilded Age. Cornelius Vanderbilt, Jim Fisk, Daniel Drew, Jay Gould, and others made fortunes and enemies as they fought for control of the Erie Railroad, the New York Central, and the Union Pacific, by manipulating the market and other dubious practices. They even tried to corner the nation's supply of gold.

Though their operations were generally not illegal at the time, they were disruptive, and despised by muckraking journalists and the American public.

This 1884 cartoon depicts robber baron Jay Gould awash in a pool of watered stocks (their value diluted by manipulative practices) while William H. Vanderbilt looks on from the steps of the Custom House.

As the investment banker's importance to the capital-raising process increased, so did his influence. Bankers started getting involved in the management of the corporations whose securities they underwrote, often demanding seats on the board of directors. The investment banker's controlling hand was usually a stabilizing force, bringing order to the capitalization and management of railroads, industrial corporations, and public utilities. Still, alarm that such concentrated power was in the hands of a few Wall Street bankers gave rise to conspiracy theories and public criticism that spurred government investigations.

Wall Street's financial power acted like a magnet, drawing other national and international corporations to the prestigious business district. Before 1890, only about a third of all U.S. railroad companies had offices in New York, but by 1900 nearly all were headquartered here, close to the investment bankers and capital markets that had become so important to their viability. Likewise, telephone and telegraph companies, such as Western Union, AT&T (NW2), and ITT (BB23) directed their vast communications networks from Lower Manhattan. Standard Oil (BB11), U.S. Steel (BB17c), and other giant industrial corporations set up corporate headquarters on lower Broadway, far removed from oil field and factory floor. In 1913 Congress created a central bank, the Federal Reserve, to regulate the nation's currency and credit. Its most important branch was located in New York, in the heart of the downtown financial district (NW29).

Although the machinations of the robber barons and investment bankers ignited the imagination and ire of the common citizen, he or she had little direct interaction with Wall Street until the country entered World War I. To finance the fight, the U.S. government raised $23 million by selling war bonds in denominations as small as ten dollars. Silent-screen stars Douglas Fairbanks and Mary Pickford urged citizens to buy the Liberty Loan bonds at huge rallies on Wall Street and all over America. All five war-bond issues were oversubscribed to by the public. For the first time, the small investor had first-

hand knowledge of what a bond was and what investment meant.

This new knowledge ill served some citizens who
plunged headlong into the speculative euphoria of the
Roaring Twenties, when economic prosperity, industrial innovation, and popular excess lifted the stock market to unheard-of heights. Over the decade, the Dow
Jones Industrial Average rose nearly sixfold. In 1928, the
price of Radio Corporation of America, the era's favorite
glamour stock, jumped from $85 to $420 a share. Stock
prices climbed steadily higher, and even sober econo-
mists opined that the market had reached a new permanent plateau. It seemed that everyone was making a
killing in the market — even the shoeshine boy had a
hot stock tip.

Optimistic investors
flocked to the stock
market during the
Roaring Twenties
only to have their
hopes and margin
accounts deflated in
the 1929 crash.

It all came crashing down, of course, on October 29, 1929 — still remembered as the biggest event in stock market history. The Dow Jones Industrial Average plunged thirty points on volume of 16 million shares, statistics that seem minuscule now but were record-setters in their day. The crash wiped out some $15 billion of market value, losses that worsened as the market continued to decline over the next three years. The stunning plunge was an indication of broad underlying economic problems: overextended credit, speculative excess, foreign-trade imbalances, and structural inadequacies in the financial markets. The Crash of 1929 marked the threshold of the Great Depression — long, difficult years of economic hardship for nearly everyone. Wall Street took it on the chin in public opinion.

A significant effect of the 1929 Crash was the introduction of government regulation into Wall Street's business. Although Congress had investigated banking and securities practices in the 1912 Money Trust Investigation, real reform came as part of New Deal legislation during the 1930s. The Banking Act of 1933, commonly called the Glass-Steagall Act, separated commercial banking (taking deposits and making loans) from investment banking (underwriting and trading securities) and created the Federal Deposit Insurance Corporation (FDIC) to protect customers' bank deposits. The Securities Act of 1933 required companies to register their stock offerings and disclose financial information to prospective investors. The following year, the Securities Exchange Commission was created to oversee practices in the stock market. Coupled with internal Wall Street reforms, federal regulation sought to rebuild public confidence in the financial markets.

The businesses of Lower Manhattan continued to make innovations during the twentieth century. New York was still the world's busiest port for the first half of the century, although its center had shifted from the downtown piers to Chelsea and Brooklyn. Eventually the shipping business would be overtaken by truck traffic and containerized shipping facilities in New Jersey. Banking developed into a more consumer-oriented business as banks opened branch offices in other New York neighborhoods and in the suburbs, and began offering consumers loans and credit cards. By mid-century, many banks had begun to move their headquarters north to Midtown, though some kept large offices in the financial district. Likewise, insurance companies started catering to the consumer, building on a tradition of offering life insurance policies to working-class families for small weekly premiums. They also became more socially active, distributing information about hygiene and nutrition to policyholders, offering visiting nurse services, and even building model housing developments for low- and moderate-income families. Insurance companies began writing lower-cost "multiple line" policies that bundled together homeowners', auto, life, and health policies. The stock market remained in the doldrums for many years following the Crash of 1929. Only World War II production needs lifted the nation out of depression, leading to a postwar economic boom. Even so, only 6.5 million Americans owned stocks in 1952. A public education and advertising campaign sponsored by the New York Stock Exchange helped lift that number to 31 million by 1970.

At mid-century women began making their mark in the financial district, still viewed by many as a gray-flannel male bastion. Although Chase National Bank had appointed a woman officer, Mary Andress, as early as 1924, women's careers in finance advanced slowly. Women worked for the first time on the New York Stock Exchange trading floor during World War II — Wall Street's corollary to Rosie the Riveter — but returned to their clerical positions when servicemen returned to work at the war's end. Banks were the biggest employers of female workers in the U.S. in 1947, but only 1 percent of high-level management jobs were held by women. Professional women were a rarity on Wall Street until the 1970s. But there were exceptions, like Josephine Bay, named chairman and president of A. M. Kidder & Company in 1956, the first woman to head a brokerage firm. Another pioneer was Muriel Siebert, who became the first woman member

of the New York Stock Exchange in 1967 and then went on to become the Superintendent of Banking for New York State. Today women's careers in finance mirror their experience and achievement in other fields.

The stock market again struck a chord in popular culture during the bull market of the 1980s. Junk bonds and leveraged buyouts somehow became glamorous in a culture dominated by yuppies. Tom Wolfe chronicled the high-flying lives and careers of Wall Street traders — "Masters of the Universe"— in his novel *The Bonfire of the Vanities*, and Oliver Stone made a moralizing movie titled *Wall Street*. The market suffered another crisis with the market break of October 19, 1987, when the Dow plunged more than 500 points—22 percent of its value. Though the losses were astounding, they were temporary. The stock market rebounded, with the Dow regaining all its losses within two years and continuing the trend upward. The crisis resulted in the merger of many financial firms, corporate downsizing, and other forms of economic belt-tightening that set the market up to begin one of history's most dramatic bull markets during the 1990s. Merger activity continued as consumers demanded one-stop shopping for their financial needs. The original intentions of the Glass-Steagall Act were diluted as diverse financial services such as banking, brokerage, and insurance were brought together under a single big umbrella.

This consolidation, as well as the migration of many firms from Lower Manhattan to Midtown, or out of Manhattan entirely, contributed to a slackening real estate market downtown, spurring the redevelopment of Lower Manhattan into a mixed-use business and residential neighborhood. Although the 1970 census recorded only 834 people living south of Chambers Street, in twenty years the population had increased to 14,000, half of them living in the large Battery Park City apartment complex. The residential population continues to grow as commercial office buildings such as the Empire Building (BB17c), once the headquarters of U.S. Steel, are converted into loft-like apartments. In a business district that had usually been deserted after 6 p.m., there are still precious few amenities of a residential neighborhood, such as grocery stores and dry cleaners. It is still too early to tell whether this diversifying trend will continue and substantially alter the character of the financial district. Even as the American Stock Exchange and its parent, the National Association of Securities Dealers, eye flashier Times Square locations, the New York Stock Exchange has decided to build a large new trading facility on the block directly opposite its Broad Street headquarters. Its continuing presence will very likely ensure that finance will continue to play a dominant role in the Wall Street area. Yet there are signs of change. Stockbrokers in power suits now share the sidewalk with new neighbors out walking their dogs along Wall Street.

A Note on the Tours

In area, Lower Manhattan is not a very large geographic section of New York City. However, its narrow streets contain one of the densest concentrations of architecturally and historically significant structures to be found anywhere. The three tours in this book wend their ways through the irregular street pattern south of Fulton Street. The walk includes the early commercial buildings of the South Street Seaport area, the early skyscrapers of lower Broadway, the great towers of the 1930s that rise from some of the narrowest streets in the district, the International style office buildings and plazas of the post-World War II era, and many other public and private structures. The tours often run very close to one another. Thus, if the walker wishes, he or she can easily move from tour to tour. The tour entries are accompanied by historical photographs and, in a few cases, by architectural drawings. These have been chosen to compliment the entries, permitting you to compare historical images with the present condition of a building or streetscape. They will also aid armchair tourists in their appreciation of the architecture of the area.

As you walk around in Lower Manhattan, you will notice many plaques elaborating on the history of the area. In particular, look for the beautifully illustrated sidewalk panels placed throughout the area by Heritage Trails New York, an organization established to increase awareness of the glories of Lower Manhattan. These panels often complement the entries in this book. Buildings which are also discussed on Heritage Trails panels are marked with the Heritage Trails logo. Each tour is followed by a few examples of Heritage Trails site markers. The text for these panels was written by Anthony Robins.

While taking the tours there are a few things that you should keep in mind. When looking at a building, you may find that you can see more if you stand on the opposite side of the street where a comprehensive view of a structure and its setting can be had. You may wish, however, to get close to a building to examine details. Since ornament on the upper floors of skyscrapers is often difficult to see, you might consider bringing along a pair of binoculars. Most buildings on the tours have been named for their original owner. Current building names are provided where applicable. The indices should aid in finding a particular structure or historic site. Many interiors of great distinction can be found in Lower Manhattan, notably banking halls and office-building lobbies. The best interiors are discussed and are often illustrated as well. Many are only open to the public during the work week. Please remember that almost all of these interiors are private property and many forbid the use of cameras.

Battery, Broadway, and Broad

This tour begins where New York began, at the southern tip of Manhattan Island, where the original colonial-era fort that housed government offices and protected the small settlement of New Amsterdam was located. Almost the entire tour route traverses the generally narrow, irregular streets laid out during the 17th and 18th centuries in Dutch-colonial New Amsterdam and English-colonial New York. One of the fascinating things about New York is that the great skyscrapers of the nation's financial capital rise along the streets of a modest colonial settlement. This tour exemplifies the variety of architecture in Lower Manhattan, from small-scale commercial buildings, to grand public monuments, to towering skyscrapers, many erected for the industrial corporations, shipping conglomerates, and banks that transformed American society.

Start: Flagpole at entrance to Battery Park.

BB1 Netherlands Memorial Flagpole
Entrance to Battery Park near intersection of State Street and Whitehall Street (H.A. Van den Eyden, 1926). A gift from the Dutch government, this flagpole commemorates the 400th anniversary of the Dutch "purchase" of Manhattan Island from the Indians in 1626 and the continuing friendship between the people of the Netherlands and those of New York City. The design on the base incorporates inscriptions in English and Dutch, carved in a popular early-20th-century Dutch graphic style; an image of Fort Amsterdam and its surroundings; and a relief of Peter Minuit handing over $24 worth of trinkets to an Indian.

Walk a few yards to the south.

BB2 Interborough Rapid Transit Company's Bowling Green Station Control House
State Street, south of Battery Place (Heins & La Farge, 1904-05). The New York City subway system was origi-

46

nally built and run by a private company, the Interborough Rapid Transit Company (IRT), operating on a long-term franchise granted by the city. The IRT was organized in 1902 to operate the city's first subway, which ran north from City Hall into the Bronx; the original fare, which lasted into the 1950's, was a nickel. Even before the first line opened in 1904, the IRT had started construction on an extension south through the financial district, including stops at Wall Street (WS2) and Bowling Green. Faced with increasing costs and competition from other subway lines, the IRT went bankrupt in 1932. In 1940 the city took over operations. The Bowling Green station has always been entered through this small but impressive "control house." The Dutch-inspired design was appropriate for a site at the edge of colonial New Amsterdam.

⊞ BB3 Battery Park

In the 1680s the British colonial government erected a battery of cannon along the waterfront, then located approximately at what is now the west side of State Street. The associated rampart, with its spectacular harbor views, soon became the city's most popular promenade. The present Battery Park is built almost entirely on landfill, most dating from the 19th century, but it still retains an impressive waterside esplanade, recently restored by the Conservancy for Historic Battery Park, a public-private stewardship group.

BB4 Castle Clinton

Battery Park (Lieutenant Colonel Jonathan Williams and John McComb, Jr., 1808-11). Despite the fact that no shot was ever fired at an enemy from this D-shaped fort (one of several erected to protect New York Harbor as tensions rose between Britain and the United States), the modest stone building has a rich and varied history. Known until 1815 as West Battery, the fort was initially built on an artificial island connected to the Battery by a wooden drawbridge. In 1823 the obsolete fort was ceded to New York City, which leased the property to a group that converted it into Castle Garden, a popular

Head down the straight walk, known as Emma Lazarus Walk, that begins at the Netherlands Memorial Flagpole, passing Hope Garden and *The Immigrants*, sculpted by Luis Sanguino in 1980, to Castle Clinton.

47

Walk along the north side of Castle Clinton (or alternatively, walk straight through the fort) to the waterside promenade, where you can see the inner harbor and, from left to right (south to north), Brooklyn, Governors Island (with the three-tiered round fortification known as Castle William), Staten Island, Liberty Island, Ellis Island, and New Jersey. Turn right and walk north along the promenade past the powerful *American Merchant Mariners' Memorial* by sculptor Marisol, installed in 1991.

Face northeast toward the city and look up.

open-air resort. In 1844 an enormous addition was erected above the fort to house a theater (famous as the site of "Swedish Nightingale" Jenny Lind's American debut in 1850). Between 1855 and 1890, Castle Garden served as the landing depot for almost eight million immigrants. With the decision to build Ellis Island, the immigrant station was closed and the building was converted into an aquarium (expanded by McKim, Mead & White in 1924-27). When New York's public works czar Robert Moses proposed the demolition of the old fort for the construction of a Brooklyn-Battery bridge, he set off a major preservation battle that culminated with the federal acquisition of the property in 1946, the demolition of all additions, and a restoration of the original fort.

BB5 Pier A
Battery Park and Battery Place (George Sears Greene, Jr., engineer, 1884-86; headhouse extension, John A. Bensel, engineer, 1900; third story, 1904). Most New York piers are numbered, but in 1883 a pier was authorized south of Pier 1 for use by the harbor police and the Department of Docks, and it was named Pier A. Pier A is the oldest surviving pier along the Manhattan waterfront and retains the only 19th-century pier shed in the city. The survival of the pier is due to its continuing use and to its durable construction of granite, concrete, and iron, with a wooden shed clad in galvanized metal. At the harbor side of the pier is a 70-foot-tall tower with a four-faced clock that chimes ship's time, installed in 1919 as a memorial to American servicemen who had died in World War I. The city-owned pier has been leased to a private developer and is being restored and renovated to house restaurants and a visitor's center for the New York State Harbor Park.

BB6 Whitehall Building
17 Battery Place (Henry Hardenbergh, 1902-04; addition, Clinton & Russell, 1908-10). The original Whitehall Building, the relatively small structure on Battery Place, with its limestone base and bays of ocher and

pinkish-red brick, occupies one of the best office building sites in New York City, with unexcelled harbor
views and unimpeded natural light. So successful was
this speculative office building that it was enlarged five-
fold only a few years after its completion with the construction of the taller addition to the rear, crowned by a
prominent terra-cotta arch supported by four crouching
figures. The building's location on landfill, with the
waterline only a few feet below ground, required a
waterproof concrete basement with walls seven feet
thick.

BB7 Brooklyn-Battery Tunnel Ventilation Building

Battery Place between Washington and Greenwich
streets (Aymar Embury II, 1940-50). Four massive limestone ventilating towers circulate air through the Brooklyn-Battery Tunnel, the longest underwater tunnel in the
world at the time of its completion. The Art Deco ventilating tower on Battery Place was enshrined in popular
culture in 1996 when it appeared as the headquarters
building in the popular film *Men in Black*.

*Battery Park with,
from left, Castle Clin-
ton with Aquarium
addition, Pier A,
Whitehall Building,
and elevated railroad
tracks, c.1910.*

**Proceed east on
Battery Place,
passing the
Whitehall Building**

**Continue east.
Cross State Street
and walk onto the
plaza.**

⊞ BB8 Bowling Green

This small space, located just outside the walls of the
colonial fort, was initially the city's meat market, but in
1733 was leased for ten years, at a fee of one peppercorn
per year, to three prominent local residents who agreed
to maintain a bowling green. In 1771 the Common
Council enclosed the park with an iron fence, since the
small open space had become "a recipticle [sic] of all the
filth and dirt of the neighborhood." This fence still surrounds the park and is one of the few surviving 18th-
century elements in New York's streetscape. The present
fountain and landscaping are the work of M. Paul Fried-
berg & Associates (1978).

*Bowling Green,
c.1895. Buildings
are being demolished
for construction of
Bowling Green Offices
at left.*

⊞ BB9 United States Custom House

Now Alexander Hamilton U.S. Custom House/The
Smithsonian Institution's National Museum of the
American Indian, George Gustav Heye Center (Cass
Gilbert, 1899-1907). Before moving into this spectacular building in 1907, the Customs Service had occupied
two other great New York City landmarks — Federal
Hall (WS5) and the Merchants' Exchange (WS12), both
on Wall Street. At the turn of the century, before the
establishment of the income tax, over three-quarters of
the income of the U. S. government was derived from

customs duties paid at New York's Custom House. Thus, when the Customs Service outgrew the Merchants' Exchange, a new structure was planned that would reflect both the importance of the Port of New York and the grandeur of the federal government. Architect Cass Gilbert won a design competition with a dynamic French Beaux-Arts work that is richly detailed, on both the exterior and interior, with symbolic and allegorical ornament. The facade is embellished with fish heads (beneath the third-story windows), tridents (the fork-like symbol of Neptune, Roman god of the sea, found along the roofline), heads representing the peoples of the world (above the second-story windows), and symbols of Mercury, Roman god of commerce (heads with winged helmets in the column capitals and caducei — staffs entwined with snakes — in the first-floor window brackets). At the top of the building are figures by various sculptors that represent great seafaring powers — from left to right, Greece, Rome, Phoenicia, Genoa (Christopher Columbus), Venice (a doge), Spain (Queen Isabella), Holland (Peter Stuyvesant), Portugal, Denmark, Belgium (originally Germany, but stripped of

The Historic Street Plan of New Amsterdam and New York

One of the most remarkable aspects of New York is the fact that the skyscrapers of America's financial center rise along the unplanned, irregular, and often extremely narrow streets that developed organically in 17th-century Dutch-colonial New Amsterdam and 18th-century English-colonial New York. New Amsterdam extended as far north as Wall Street, with the original waterfront at Pearl, State, and Greenwich streets. The two widest streets were Broadway, an old Indian trail known as Wickquasgeck, extending north along a natural ridge; and Broad Street, where an inlet was turned into a canal (filled and paved in 1676) flanked by two streets. The irregular pattern of streets led to such anomalous features as the juncture of William, South William, and Beaver streets, creating several oddly shaped building plots.

Teutonic detail during World War I), England, and France. The most important sculptures are Daniel Chester French's *Four Continents*, carved from Tennessee marble. Dynamic America and regal Europe command prime locations flanking the entrance, while contemplative Asia and sleeping Africa are at the far ends of the building.

The Customs Service vacated this building in 1973, and the U.S. Bankruptcy Court remained its sole occupant for many years. The lower floors were restored by Ehrenkrantz & Eckstut, and became a branch of the Smithsonian Institution's Museum of the American Indian in 1994. Enter the building by walking up the grand staircase, beneath the mosaic barrel vault. Straight ahead is the Rotunda, one of the finest Beaux-Arts rooms in America, a skylit oval ornamented with sea symbols. Reginald Marsh's mural cycle illustrating the progress of several ships as they enter New York Harbor (reporters interview Greta Garbo in one scene) was added as part of a Depression-era federal works project in 1937.

U.S. Custom House rotunda with Reginald Marsh's murals, c.1940s.

BB10 International Mercantile Marine Company Building

1 Broadway, northwest corner Battery Place (Walter B. Chambers, 1919-21). The creation of the severe Neoclassical facade of the former headquarters of the International Mercantile Marine Company (IMM) is the result of one of the more fascinating office-building construction projects in New York City. This was the site of the red-brick Washington Building, (see photograph, p.56) a pioneering effort at tall-building construction, erected in 1882-87. When IMM acquired the property in 1919 there were many long-term office leases, so the company chose not to demolish the old structure, but rather had Walter B. Chambers design new limestone street facades and modernized interiors.

Walk to the corner of Broadway and Battery Place.

IMM was organized in 1902 by J. P. Morgan (see p. 89) in an attempt to curb competition in transatlantic shipping. The company merged five principal British and American steamship lines, including the American and White Star lines. Morgan was unable to find a market for the enormous holding company's securities, resulting in big losses for the underwriting syndicate. With a fleet of 136 vessels, IMM was the world's largest steamship company. However, it was never profitable, and the sinking of the White Star Line's Titanic in 1912 was an added financial disaster. IMM's principal subsidiary, the United States Lines, continued operating well into the 1960s and retained ownership of this building until 1979.

Appropriately, the exterior of the IMM Building is embellished with nautical motifs — notably, mosaic coats-of-arms of prominent ports, lamps with tridents, and, at the main entrance, figures of Mercury and Neptune and carved sea shells and starfish. The entrances on Battery Place, marked "First Class" and "Cabin Class," lead into the former ticketing office (now a Citibank branch, open during banking hours and visible at all times from the ATM area). This luxurious room, reminiscent of the ballroom of an 18th-century country house, contains curved, apsidal ends marked by black-marble columns, iron balcony railings emblazoned with the IMM monogram, marble floor compasses, wall murals, and elegant lamps in the form of early ship's lanterns.

Standard Oil Building, after completion of first three sections, 1923. Original Standard Oil Building, at left, would have its facade replaced in 1924–25. Note Child's Restaurant building in light court at right.

BB11 Standard Oil Building

26 Broadway, northeast corner Beaver Street (Carrère & Hastings; Shreve, Lamb & Blake, associate architect, 1920-28). Standard Oil's founder, John D. Rockefeller got his start in the oil business in Cleveland during the Civil War. In 1870 he organized the Standard Oil Company of Ohio and quickly built it into a vertically integrated monopoly controlling virtually every phase of petroleum production and distribution. The company owned extensive oil fields in the Midwest, operated a host of refineries, manufactured its own barrels, owned a network of oil pipelines, managed seaport oil terminals, commanded a fleet of oceangoing tankers, and delivered kerosene to its customers' doors in horse-drawn Standard Oil tank wagons. The company also pioneered new forms of corporate organization, first concentrating control of its many enterprises in a trust, a device so widely emulated that the term came to mean nearly any kind of industrial monopoly. Later, in 1899, it created the Standard Oil Company of New Jersey, a holding company that effectively controlled the vast Rockefeller empire. An antitrust decision against the company in 1911 compelled it to distribute to stockholders its holdings in 33 oil-refining and pipeline companies. Even so, in 1920 Standard Oil owned or controlled 29 petroleum companies in the United States, Europe, and Mexico, producing 31 million barrels of naphtha, gasoline, and refined fuel and lubricating oils. In 1972 the company changed its name to Exxon Corporation and in 1999 merged with Mobil Oil (originally Standard Oil of New York), reuniting two large pieces of the Standard Oil empire.

Befitting its position as one of the most powerful corporations in America, Standard Oil commissioned a conservative building on one of the most prominent sites in Lower Manhattan. The facade of the impressive limestone-clad skyscraper gently curves, following the course of Broadway, and rises through a series of setbacks to a tower crowned by a Classical-inspired brazier that is highly visible from the harbor. Construction was organized in five stages so that tenants in buildings on

After visiting the interior of the International Mercantile Marine Building, return to Broadway. Look up and to the east, across Bowling Green.

the site, including Standard Oil staff, would not be unduly inconvenienced. One hitch occurred when the owner of a Child's restaurant (an early chain restaurant) on Beaver Street refused to vacate until his lease expired in 1928. The great skyscraper was erected around and partially over his small five-story, 22-foot-wide building, which was later demolished and its site filled in, thus accounting for the light court on the building's south facade. The building has an impressive lobby (it can be conveniently visited later on the tour), where, as a 1932 guidebook noted, "one can almost feel the presence of John D. Rockefeller." The lobby walls are inscribed with the names of founders of the company (John D. Rockefeller's name is carved above a pedestal that once supported his portrait bust).

Cross Broadway and walk north along the west side of Bowling Green.

Excavations for U.S. Custom House, with Washington Building and Bowling Green Offices at rear, c.1900.

BB12 Bowling Green Offices

11 Broadway (W. & G. Audsley, 1895-98). Only a few years after the completion of the modest Tower Building, New York's first skeleton-frame skyscraper (see p. 61), massive buildings such as this were appearing in Lower Manhattan. The Scottish-immigrant architects of the Bowling Green Offices, brothers who also designed

organ cases, referred to its style as "Hellenic Renaissance," defined as "a free but pure treatment of ancient Greek architecture." This is especially evident at the base.

Continue north onto the small plaza just north of Bowling Green.

BB13 *Charging Bull*

(Arturo Di Modica, sculptor, 1989). During the night of December 15, 1989, without authorization from city officials, Arturo Di Modica installed this sculpture in the middle of Broad Street, outside the New York Stock Exchange — an appropriate site, since the bull is the symbol of an optimistic investor. The sculpture was removed by the city the next day, but the public's affection for the piece led authorities to find a home for it here. A favorite with tourists, the bull's head is buffed to a shine by people posing for photographs.

Cross the eastern branch of Broadway to visit the Standard Oil lobby. Then look across to the west side of Broadway.

BB14 Cunard Building

25 Broadway, southwest corner Morris Street (Benjamin Wistar Morris; Carrère & Hastings, consulting architect, 1917-21). Cunard, the venerable British steamship line, was established in 1839 when Canadian Samuel Cunard won a British government contract to initiate regular steamship mail service between Great Britain and North America. The company was organized as the British and North American Royal Mail Steam Packet Company in 1840 and began fortnightly voyages from Liverpool to Nova Scotia. By 1847, the Company had designated New York City its main American port. Cunard was the first to offer scheduled transatlantic passenger service — aboard the *Britannia*, a wooden paddle-wheel steamer that could accommodate 115 first-class passengers. The ship made its first crossing in 1840 in the relatively speedy time of 14 days, 8 hours. During the late 19th century and much of the 20th century, the Cunard Line was famous for offering stylish first-class travel to wealthy passengers on such legendary liners as the Mauretania, the Queen Mary, and the Queen Elizabeth. To many more immigrants headed to America, it provided less luxurious third-class "steerage" accommodations.

Cunard established a real estate subsidiary to build its

Cunard Booking Hall with frescoes by Ezra Winter, 1921. The bronze floor roundel, now hidden, is the work of John Gregory.

American headquarters, a building that would include a ticket-booking hall, office space for the company and its subsidiaries (Cunard initially occupied the lower four floors and the top of the building), and extensive rental space. The severe Italian Renaissance-inspired limestone exterior, with its subtle nautical ornamentation, contrasts with the richness of the interior, which the magazine *Architecture and Building* described in 1921 as "the most imposingly beautiful hall which has ever been created for the booking of transatlantic passengers and freight." The interior, entered through the three central arches, is open during post office hours.

Cross Broadway to visit the interior of the Cunard Building.

Visitors first encounter a vestibule with a ceiling sculpted by Carl Jennewein and painted by Ezra Winter, adorned with nautical images, many quite whimsical. Samuel Yellin's hand-wrought iron gates (see p. 142) provide access to the booking hall. The booking hall for first- and second-class tickets (third-class tickets were purchased in the basement) is a complex and magnificent space with travertine walls and a travertine and marble floor. The Italian Renaissance style ceiling frescoes, modeled after those at the Villa Madama in Rome, are the work of Ezra Winter, who wrote that they portray "the age-old romance of the sea or lure of travel." In the central octagon are the ships of four great ocean explorers — Leif Ericson, Christopher Columbus, Sebastian Cabot, and Francis Drake — "in a sense the forerunners of the Cunard steamships which travel some of the same ocean routes." In addition, Barry Faulkner painted murals of Cunard's shipping routes on the walls of side niches. White travertine counters originally ran around the space but were reconfigured by the U.S. Postal Service in 1974. A post office could be a fine reuse for this space, but the present intrusive design is not compatible with the magnificence of the original concept.

Leave the Cunard Building and turn left. Walk north on Broadway to the corner of Morris Street.

BB15 29 Broadway

Northwest corner Morris Street (Sloan & Robertson, 1929-31). This handsome but often overlooked Art Deco office building, with its exceptionally narrow frontage on Broadway, was a purely speculative venture. The exterior, faced in white marble and brick, is carefully massed to balance horizontal bands of windows, accented with dark brickwork, with vertical marble piers outlined in stylized Deco detail. Don't overlook the long, narrow lobby, entered through an outer vestibule with silver mosaic ceiling and original chandelier. The dynamic veining of the Greek marble walls of the lobby guides the visitor toward the elevator banks. Take special note of the aluminum grilles, directory board, elevator doors, and, most especially, the magnificent mailbox with its modern (for 1931) ship, train, and airplane.

Cross to the east side of Broadway and look back at 29 Broadway and the Harriman Building.

BB16 Harriman Building

39 Broadway (Cross & Cross, 1926-28). This skyscraper, with its dramatic setbacks and expressive brick

patterning, was erected during a boom period when Lower Manhattan was, according to one contemporary source, "experiencing one of the greatest building programs it has ever known." The building is closely associated with the early business and financial career of W. Averell Harriman. Harriman, son of railroad magnate E. H. Harriman, had early business success in railroads, shipping, and finance. Two of his banking concerns, W. A. Harriman & Company and Harriman Brothers & Company, were merged with Brown Brothers in 1931 and moved into that firm's new building on Wall Street (WS14). Harriman's subsequent record of public service was long and distinguished: ambassador to the USSR, ambassador to Great Britain, secretary of commerce, and governor of New York.

Walk north on Broadway to Exchange Place. Look at the three early skyscrapers on the west side of Broadway between Exchange Alley and Rector Street.

BB17a Adams Express Building

61 Broadway, northwest corner Exchange Alley (Francis H. Kimball, 1912-16); **BB17b American Express Building**, 65 Broadway (Renwick, Aspinwall & Tucker, 1916-17); and **BB17c Empire Building** 71 Broadway, southwest corner Rector Street (Kimball & Thompson, 1895-98). These three tall skyscrapers, each rising without setbacks, illustrate the scale of office buildings erected before the passage of the 1916 zoning law (see p. 125). The designs, two by noted skyscraper architect Francis H. Kimball (see p. 120), took advantage of developments in steel- frame construction, foundation engineering (a necessity in an area where quicksand and river water were commonly encountered during excavations), and wind bracing. Light was also of great importance in the days before fluorescent fixtures, accounting, for example, for the slender court that splits the facade of the midblock American Express Building. Architecturally, the most distinguished of the three is the Empire Building, with its triumphal-arch entrance and Renaissance detail . From 1901 until 1976 this was the headquarters of the United States Steel Corporation. U.S. Steel was formed in 1901 by the combination of Andrew Carnegie's huge steel concern with seven other steel manufacturers. The merger was engineered by

J. P. Morgan (see p. 89) and resulted in the world's first corporation capitalized at $1 billion, greater even than the budget of the U.S. government at the time. The deal made Carnegie the richest man in the world and allowed him to retire and pursue an ambitious philanthropic career that created thousands of public libraries and supported many other educational and public works projects.

The two other buildings originally housed the headquarters offices of express companies. Express companies first sprang up during the 1840s, just as America's transportation infrastructure of roads, rail lines, and canals was being built. People relied on express compa-

Tower Building

The first skyscraper in New York (and perhaps the first in the world) to employ a skeleton frame rose at 50 Broadway in 1888-89 and survived only until 1914. This was the extraordinarily narrow Tower Building, with its Broadway frontage measuring only 21 feet. The plot was so skinny that had the developer erected a traditional building with masonry walls bearing the weight of the structure, each side wall would have had to be three feet thick, leaving little room for the lobby, elevators, stairs, and income-producing offices. Thus, architect Bradford Gilbert devised an iron frame to support the walls and floors on the first six stories of the eleven-story building (he employed traditional wall-bearing construction on the upper stories, where the walls could be less thick). The success of the innovative structural system in the construction of this traditionally styled Romanesque Revival building led directly to an explosion of enormous skeleton-frame skyscrapers on Broadway and adjoining streets, including the Bowling Green Offices (BB12), Empire Building (BB17c), and Broad-Exchange Building (BB18).

Adams Express, American Express, and Empire buildings, with Trinity Church at right.

nies for regular, speedy, and secure transportation of valuable goods, documents, and money, particularly to the uncharted western territories, where travel was inconvenient and hazardous. The express companies soon began to offer ancillary financial services to travelers and western pioneers. The most important early express company, Adams & Company, was formed in 1840. During the Gold Rush of 1849, Adams set up offices in 35 California towns and mining camps and dominated the transport of gold back east. At mid-century the company was a strong competitor to American Express in the east and Wells, Fargo & Co. in the west.

American Express was founded in 1850 by two legendary names: Henry Wells and William G. Fargo. The company first entered the financial services sector in 1882 when it introduced its own money order, selling nearly 12,000 in the first six weeks. In 1891 American

Express invented the traveler's cheque, whose phenomenal success inspired the company to open a network of offices throughout the world offering a variety of travel services. American Express launched its famous credit card in 1958 while still headquartered in this building.

Turn right on Exchange Place. Cross New Street and continue to Broad Street.

BB18 Broad-Exchange Building

Now The Exchange, 25 Broad Street, southeast corner Exchange Place (Clinton & Russell, 1899-1902). At the time of its completion, this was the largest office building in the world, with 326,500 square feet of floor space. It exemplifies speculative construction, having been built by a syndicate of investors who intended to maximize rental floor space without expending an inordinately large amount of money on extraneous ornamentation. They hired the firm of Clinton & Russell which specialized in this type of speculative skyscraper design. The twenty-story building appears from the street to be a rectangular box articulated by evenly spaced office windows, each pair lighting an individual office. High-quality materials were employed in a manner that adds interest to the facades, but except at the Classical entrances there is little additional detailing. As was typical of a speculative office buildings, Clinton & Russell designed an impressive lobby with marble columns and walls and extensive decorative detailing. The building was in the vanguard of the movement in the 1990s to convert obsolete office buildings in Lower Manhattan into housing.

Broad-Excahnge Building as illustrated on a postcard printed shortly after its comletion.

BB19 Lee, Higginson & Company Building

41 Broad Street (Cross & Cross), 1928-29). Lee, Higginson & Company, an unfamiliar name on Wall Street today, was among the top tier of important investment banks during the late 19th and early 20th centuries. Founded in Boston in 1848, the firm originally served a small clientele of New England capitalists who gave the firm access to a large, steady stream of funds. During the heyday of railroad stock trading, Lee, Higginson was an early underwriter of industrial corporations. With J. P. Morgan & Company, the firm financed the merger that

Turn right and walk a few yards south on Broad Street.

created the General Electric Company in 1892. The firm was also one of the earliest to cater to the small investor, building a formidable retail sales network that marketed bonds and stocks of utilities and industrial companies to individuals. Lee, Higginson was among a small group of private banks that could afford to build modestly-scaled headquarters structures on enormously expensive pieces of land. However, only a few years after the building's construction, the bank's reputation was tarnished owing to its involvement with one of the great financial scandals of the era — the fraudulent manipulations of European financier and industrialist Ivar Kreuger, whose career of embezzlement and forgery ended when he shot himself in a Paris hotel. Lee, Higginson continued business until it was folded into Hayden, Stone in 1966.

The Curb Market

Broad Street at the beginning of the 20th century served as the trading floor for a hardy group of stockbrokers known collectively as the Curb Market. With a genealogy stretching back to the 1790s,

the "curbstone brokers" traded in the open air of the street and specialized in the more speculative stocks of emerging industries and young companies. Unable to meet the membership requirements of the New York Stock Exchange, the curb brokers traded in its shadow in all kinds of weather. Their phone clerks, perched in second- and third-story office windows along Broad Street, communicated customers' orders to the brokers in the street below by means of hand signals. In 1921 the curb brokers shook the dust of the street off their heels and moved indoors to a new building two blocks away, changing their name in 1953 to the American Stock Exchange (still located at 86 Trinity Place).

Shortly after the completion of this headquarters building, *Banker's Magazine* described the Neo-Greek style structure as "one of the finest examples of architectural beauty in New York City." Indeed, this is a fascinating building worthy of far more attention than it has received. A smooth lower section with an austere entrance is separated from an Ionic colonnade by a band embellished with braziers, garlands, and signs of the zodiac in the form of coins. On the upper portion of the facade are relief panels, carved by the prominent

Lee, Higginson & Company Bank with murals by Griffith Baily Coale, c.1929.

sculptor Leo Friedlander, on themes such as "Transportation" (second from the left; note the modern airplane and locomotive), "Filial Fidelity" (fourth), and "Agriculture and Industry" (fifth). The stunning banking hall (presently inaccessible) is enlivened by colorful mosaic columns and Griffith Baily Coale's mural cycle illustrating the history of ships, from ancient to modern. In 2000 the building was vacant; hopefully the space will be rented to a tenant who will respect the design.

BB20 American Bureau of Shipping Building

45 Broad Street (Theodore W. Davis, 1945). The American Bureau of Shipping was created in 1862 by leaders of ten marine insurance companies. Originally known as the American Shipmasters' Association, it wrote safety standards and credentialing examinations for ship officers and seamen. The ABS developed a classification of standards for construction and operation of seagoing vessels and in 1867 began publishing a registry of ships, *The Record of American and Foreign Shipping*. The ABS is an important industry regulator that has steered development of the shipbuilding industry and maritime commerce from the early days of wooden steamships to today's containerized shipping and mobile offshore drilling rigs. In 1945 the ABS purchased a building on this site and had its facade replaced and interiors modernized. Note the ABS's American eagle symbol above the central archway. In 1978 the ABS moved out of this building.

BB21 50 Broad Street

(Willauer, Sharpe & Bready, 1912-13). In 1913 a writer for the *Real Estate Record and Builders Guide* compared the massing of this building, with its two towers separated by a light court, to "a great cathedral standing at the head of a vista." The building is clad almost entirely in white-glazed terra cotta. Note the huge pilaster capitals at the third story, from which bulls and bears peer down on the brokers and investors hurrying along Broad Street.

Continue south on Broad Street to the corner of Beaver Street.

BB22 American Bank Note Company Building

70 Broad Street, between Beaver and Marketfield streets
(Kirby, Petit & Green, 1906-08). The American Bank
Note Company was the engraver and printer of most of
the stock and bond certificates traded on Wall Street, as
well as paper currencies and postage stamps issued by
banks and governments around the world. To thwart
counterfeiters the company employed many special
processes, ranging from the aesthetic to the practical:
minutely detailed hand-engraved vignettes, lacy borders
engraved with a precise geometric lathe, and paper
embedded with tiny colored disks. All printing plates
were safeguarded in the company's burglarproof vaults.
The company's origins date back through a dozen firms
to 1795, when Robert Scot, the first engraver of the U.S.
Mint, set up business in Philadelphia. The American Bank
Note Company was formed in 1858 with the merger of
seven bank-note printers that had offices stretching from
Montreal to New Orleans. For its headquarters, the company purchased a small, but prominent site and appropriately erected a monumental granite structure in the
Classical Revival style popular for bank buildings. The
building now houses a popular restaurant, the Wall
Street Kitchen and Bar.

Cross Beaver
Street. Walk to the
corner of Market-
field Street and
look across Broad
Street.

BB23 International Telephone and Telegraph (ITT) Building

75 Broad Street (Buchman & Kahn, 1927-28; extension
Louis S. Weeks, 1929-30). Although it appears to be a
single structure, the former ITT Building was actually
erected in two campaigns. Abraham Lefcourt, one of the
most active builders of office towers during the 1920s,
commissioned Buchman & Kahn to design a tower at the
corner of Broad and Beaver streets that was to be known
as the Lefcourt Exchange Building. A few months after
construction began, ITT leased 19 of the building's 31
stories, and within a year the company had purchased
the building and adjoining plots. Louis Weeks designed
an addition that matches the original; a seam is visible
just to the left of the entrance bay. The addition includes
the main entrance; the lobby (worth a visit), with its
murals by George Davidson; and, most notably, the

ITT Building in 1928 before construction began on the addition. The Cotton Exchange (WS16) is visible at left-rear.

entrance niche on the corner of South William Street, with its mosaic half-dome by Victor White, displaying the figure of Commerce uniting the Eastern and Western Hemispheres, while balancing an electric bolt between his hands, much as ITT's international communications network knit together various regions of the globe.

The International Telephone and Telegraph Corporation was created in 1920 by two brothers, Sosthenes and Hernand Behn of Puerto Rico. They had overhauled the limping Puerto Rico Telephone Company, linked it with the phone system in Cuba and tied both systems to the continental United States with three submarine cables stretching from Havana to Key West, Florida. Over the next decade, the company created a network of local telephone and telegraph systems in 30 countries. It built a general telephone service in Spain during the 1920s, and in 1930 set up Vatican City's telephone system. Even after ITT had diversified into businesses ranging from Sheraton hotels to the Hartford Insurance Company and had become one of the world's largest multinational companies, its international communications offices remained in this building, leaving only in the 1990s.

BB24 Maritime Exchange Building
80 Broad Street (Sloan & Robertson, 1930-31). The Maritime Exchange served as a meeting place and a central clearinghouse for shipping news. The Exchange's bulletin boards, telegraph connections, library of newspapers, and shipping lists provided reports of ship's arrivals in ports around the world, cargo data, harbor information, and news of marine disasters. The Exchange, which traces its roots back to 1862, had previously occupied a small building on this site and was provided with a new space on the ground floor of this speculative office building. The building illustrates one popular way of massing a skyscraper under the 1916 zoning law (see p. 125) — placing a massive slab at the rear of a lot, with stepback wings rising from the street. The design has a great deal in common with Sloan & Robertson's contemporaneous 29 Broadway (BB15); this is evident in the ornamental detail on the exterior

Turn left on South
William Street
and walk about
three-quarters of
the way down the
block.

and in the use of heavily veined marble in the lobby.
The decoration incorporates many nautical symbols,
including the seahorses above the entrance, the sea crea-
tures on the grilles and elevator doors, the metal frieze
of sailing ships in the lobby, and the ships in the ceiling
mural by Lillian Gaertner Palmedo.

*C.P.H. Gilbert's
design for 13 South
William Street,
1903.*

BB25a 13-15 South William Street
(1836-39; new facades: No. 13, C.P.H. Gilbert, 1903;
No. 15, C.P.H. Gilbert, 1908-09); **BB25b 17 South
William Street** (1837-38; new facade, Edward L. Tilton,
1905-06); and **BB25c 21-23
South William Street** (William
Neil Smith, 1927-28). The small
buildings lining South William
Street and adjoining Stone Street
between Broad Street and
Hanover Square, now part of the
Stone Street Historic District,
form a remarkable enclave amid
the skyscrapers that define most
of Lower Manhattan. These
streets were lined with Greek
Revival style counting houses
erected after the Great Fire of
December 1835. In the early
20th century, several of the
South William Street facades
were redesigned. The earliest
and most interesting of these is
No. 13, which received a new
front designed in a style reminiscent of the Dutch houses that had
once stood on the street. The
alteration, extended to No. 15 in
1908, was commissioned by
Amos R. Eno for his family's real
estate office. The style of the
building was especially appropriate because Eno was one of the
first New Yorkers to study the

city's early history and was a collector of prints of old New York. Two years after the initial Eno project, No. 17, next door, received a medieval-inspired facade, while in 1927, a picturesque Neo-Tudor style club-house, Block Hall (note the BH monogram above the entrance), was erected to the west. On the north side of South William Street, where the garage is now located, was the site of the first synagogue in America, erected by Congregation Shearith Israel in 1728-30.

Turn right on Mill Lane and right again on Stone Street.

⬤ BB26 Stone Street

(c. 1836-37). Miraculously, the Greek Revival counting houses that were erected after the Great Fire of 1835 are largely intact along this stretch of Stone Street, although many have been neglected. If you look carefully, you can see the original granite bases through which barrels, bales, and other packages and containers were once hauled. Considerably later than these buildings is the former **Chubb & Son Building** at No. 54 (Arthur C. Jackson, 1919), headquarters of a well-known marine insurance company founded in 1882. The exposed rivets of the metal cornice and the steel window lintels provide unusual French Beaux-Arts-inspired decorative detail of a type that will be seen at the Whitehall Ferry Terminal (BB31). As part of the designation of this area as a historic district in 1996, Beyer Blinder Belle pre-pared a master plan for the restoration and economic revitalization of what could be one of the city's most beautiful building complexes. Under the auspices of the City's Landmarks Preservation Commission and the Alliance for Downtown New York, Inc., Stone Street has been closed to traffic and paved with granite Belgian blocks (NW17). Private owners plan to restore many of the buildings and convert them into housing, hotels, and other uses.

Continue along Stone Street. Cross Coenties Alley, now a paved plaza, and walk beneath the arcade of 85 Broad Street. Turn left and walk to the corner of Pearl Street.

BB27 Goldman Sachs Building

85 Broad Street (Skidmore, Owings & Merrill, 1982-83). This hulking building, not one of SOM's best designs, obliterated a section of Stone Street (memorial-ized in the curve of the elevator lobby). Archaeological

excavations on the site uncovered remains of the Lovelace Tavern, erected in 1670 by English governor Sir Francis Lovelace on a site that once faced the waterfront. The remains of the tavern are visible beneath the arcade, while an early-18th-century well is displayed nearby. The building houses the headquarters of the investment bank Goldman Sachs which was organized in 1869 by Marcus Goldman, a Bavarian immigrant. One of an important group of Wall Street banks headed by German Jews, the firm initially dealt in commercial paper, foreign exchange and stock brokerage. After the turn of the 20th century, Goldman, Sachs played a leading role in financing small manufacturers and retailers of consumer goods, floating stock issues for Sears, Roebuck and Company, F. W. Woolworth, and Macy's, among many others. The firm co-managed the initial public offering of Ford Motor Company stock in 1956, the biggest equity offering up to that time.

Look across Pearl Street, the original waterfront of Manhattan.

BB28 Fraunces Tavern Block Historic District

Unlike South William and Stone streets (BB25 and BB26), this square block escaped the ravages of the 1835 fire that destroyed much of Lower Manhattan (see p. 99), thus the block contains some of the oldest buildings in the area, including eleven erected between 1827 and 1833. The most notable of these is 62 Pearl Street (1827; third from the left), a rare surviving Federal style commercial building (probably originally also used as a residence), articulated with round-arch windows capped by paneled stone lintels. At the corner of Pearl and Broad streets is the famous Fraunces Tavern (BB29).

Cross Pearl Street, turn right and walk to the corner of Broad Street.

BB29 Fraunces Tavern

54 Pearl Street (1719; reconstruction, William H. Mersereau, 1904-07). The Fraunces Tavern Museum was established to commemorate George Washington and restore the building in which he gave his famous farewell speech to his officers in 1783. The building was erected in 1719 as the home of Stephen De Lancey. In 1762 it was sold to Samuel Fraunces, a West Indian

72

native of French extraction, who opened a restaurant
and tavern known as the Queen's Head (Pearl Street
was then known as Queen Street). Not only was the
establishment well-known for its food and drink, but it
also offered a service dear to the hearts of New Yorkers,
even in the 18th century — takeout food: a 1770 adver-
tisement offered "dinners and suppers dressed to send
out for lodgers and others who live at a convenient
distance." In 1768 the Chamber of Commerce (NW31)
was founded in the long room of the tavern, the same
setting as for Washington's speech. After Fraunces sold
the building in 1785, it underwent many changes: two
stories were added, and it was damaged in two fires.
According to Mrs. Melusina Fay Pierce, then president
of the women's auxiliary of the American Scenic and
Historic Preservation Society, by the late 19th century
Fraunces' Tavern (the apostrophe has been dropped)
was "a sad, sordid and disgraceful sight...the shabby
old corner number in a shabby old five-story
block...used as a cheap restaurant."

*Fraunces Tavern in the
late 19th century.*

Turn left on Broad Street and walk to Water Street. Cross Water Street and turn left. While walking north, look left at the view towards the towers of the Manhattan Company Building (WS9) and the City Bank-Farmers Trust Building (WS15). Turn right onto Vietnam Veterans Memorial Plaza.

Walk through the park, exit onto South Street, and turn right. Note the wonderful view to Brooklyn. Cross Broad Street.

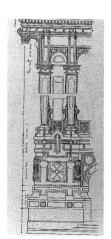

Drawing of support column for the Whitehall Ferry Terminal, c.1906.

By 1901 the Historic Preservation Society was spearheading a campaign to have the city purchase the building and convert it into a patriotic memorial where "every United States citizen might reverently stand." Although the city agreed to buy the property, it was actually purchased by the Sons of the Revolution in 1904, and they hired William Mersereau to restore the building to its condition in 1783. Some of the bricks on the second and third stories — yellow Dutch bricks on Broad Street and red bricks on Pearl Street — are original, but everything else is a reconstruction, much of it conjectural. New yellow bricks were handmade in Holland, while red bricks were manufactured in Baltimore to match the originals. Certain aspects of the project, notably the flat roof with balustrade, were quite controversial. Today, the reconstructed building is an important example of early-20th-century Colonial Revival design and is among the earliest historic preservation projects undertaken in New York.

BB30 Vietnam Veterans Memorial

Water Street at Coenties Slip (Peter Wormser and William Fellows, architects; John Ferrandino, writer, 1984-85). New York City's Vietnam Veterans Memorial is a powerful wall of glass block, lit at night, onto which are etched excerpts from letters, speeches, newspaper articles, and other writings about the war. Unfortunately, the memorial was placed on a bleak plaza, originally known as Jeannette Park. In 2000, a renovation designed by E. Timothy Marshall & Associates, was undertaken that will create a more fitting setting for the memorial.

BB31 Whitehall Ferry Terminal

Now Battery Maritime Building, 11 South Street, at the foot of Whitehall Street (Walker & Morris, 1906-09). Before bridges and tunnels linked the various parts of New York City, ferries were a crucial means of transportation for hundreds of thousands of people every day. This terminal, the last survivor of the city's historic ferry buildings, originally served ferries connecting Manhattan with 39th Street in Brooklyn. The highly decorative use of exposed steel and cast iron, with rivets, latticework, and stylized classical motifs, was inspired by French Beaux-Arts exposition architecture.

Continue along South Street and turn right on Whitehall Street. Walk to State Street, turn left.

⊞ BB32 James Watson House

Now Shrine of St. Elizabeth Ann Seton and Chapel of Our Lady of the Rosary, 7 State Street (1793; extension attributed to John McComb, 1806). No. 7 was one of a small group of late-18th-century rowhouses erected by James Watson at a time when State Street, overlooking the Battery and the harbor, was a prestigious residential address. The simple Georgian style house received an elegant Federal style addition (the slender portico columns are said to be ships' masts), the design of which is attributed to one of the architects of City Hall. Elizabeth Ann Seton, founder of the Sisters of Charity (the first order of nuns in the United States), and the first American-born Roman Catholic saint, lived on the site of the adjoining church from 1801 to 1803.

Ellis Island and the Statue of Liberty are national monuments of transcendent importance, fraternal twins celebrating America's immigrant history. The Statue of Liberty offers the ideal: the welcome extended to "the huddled masses yearning to breathe free" immortalized in Emma Lazarus's poem, chiseled in its base. Ellis Island offers the real: the gritty, difficult, miraculous place where millions of immigrants from all corners of the globe entered the New World between 1892 and 1954.

Today, one hundred million Americans can trace some part of their family history through Ellis Island. Thanks to the generosity of the American people, prompted by the fundraising efforts of the Statue of Liberty-Ellis Island Foundation, the National Park Service has restored both the Statue and Ellis Island's main building which now houses an immigration museum. Efforts are now underway to preserve and reuse the historic hospital complex on the south side of the Island.

Heritage Trails Site Marker #G13: Entrance to Battery Park at West Street and Battery Place

Big things are not unusual in New York, but even so the Statue of Liberty is special. It rises 150 feet above a huge granite base of equal height, it stands on its own island, was fabricated from 100 tons of copper hammered out to a thickness of 3/32nds of an inch, is supported by 125 tons of iron and steel, and came across the Atlantic in 214 crates. It was a gift from France in celebration of America's hundredth birthday, given in 1876. The statue of "Liberty Enlightening the World," the work of Frederic-Auguste Bartholdi, sculptor, was created in collaboration with engineering Gustave Eiffel, creator of the Eiffel Tower, and the architect for the base, Richard Morris Hunt.

A ride on the Staten Island Ferry, now free of charge, ranks as one of New York's most spectacular sight-seeing opportunities. Departing often from the South Ferry Terminal, the big orange ferryboats ply the grand confluence of the East and Hudson Rivers, passing Governors Island, the Statue of Liberty, and Ellis Island. Returning passengers get a classic view of Downtown's majestic skyline. This journey inspired the Edna St. Vincent Millay to capture the moment in her 1920's poem, "Recuardo":

We were very tired, we were very merry —
We had gone back and forth all night on the ferry.
It was bare and bright, and smelled like a stable —
But we looked into a fire, we leaned across a table,
We lay on a hill-top underneath the moon;
And the whistles kept blowing, and the dawn came soon.

We were very tired, we were very merry —
We had gone back and forth all night on the ferry.
And you ate an apple, and I ate a pear,
From a dozen of each we had bought somewhere;
And the sky went wan, and the wind came cold,
And the sun rose dripping, a bucketful of gold.

We were very tired, we were very merry —
We had gone back and forth all night on the ferry.
We hailed, "Good morrow, mother!" To a
    shawl-covered head.
And bought a morning paper, which neither of
    us read.
And she wept "God bless you!" for the apples
    and the pears.
And we gave her all our money but our subway
    fares.

Heritage Trails Site Marker #G10: Western corner of Peter Minuit Plaza, opposite South Ferry Terminal

New York is a city of straight lines — it's the very rare building that curves. The rectory of the Shrine of Elizabeth Ann Seton occupies one of them: the elegant townhouse built in 1793 for James Watson, with an 1806 addition whose portico curves along State Street. At the time, the area was a posh residential district lined with fine brick townhouses. Today, the Watson House is the sole survivor, one of the few Downtown buildings that survived the great fire of 1835. The double-story wooden columns of the curved extension are said to be made from old shipmasts.

St. Elizabeth Ann Seton, also known as Mother Seton, founded the Sisters of Charity, America's first order of nuns. In 1975, she became the first native-born American (and New Yorker) to be named a saint by the Catholic Church. Inside the shrine is a handsome and peaceful sanctuary.

Nearby, at 17 State Street, lies "New York Unearthed," where archaeological finds from New York are displayed by the South Street Seaport Museum. Unearthed castoffs of three centuries of city dwellers include: Delft tiles and clay pipes from the Dutch; patent medicine bottles from the tenements of 19th-century immigrants, and children's dolls from the early 20th century African-American community of Weeksville in Brooklyn. Lively exhibits graphically depict the layers of potential finds beneath a typical Wall Street building. And visitors can watch archeologists at work, cataloging and conserving real finds.

Heritage Trails Site Marker #G11: At 17 State Street, across the street from Peter Minuit Plaza

All visitors, whether or not they're old enough to
remember the Vietnam War, find this Memorial a powerful experience. The simple 1985 granite and glass-
block memorial, 14 feet high by 70 feet long, is
inscribed with writings. Mostly excerpts from letters
home by soldiers, some of who were killed in action,
they evoke the emotion of the war. Shelves are provided for flowers, wreaths and candles. At dusk, it is lit
from within.

Building Downtown means building on history —
literally. The office building at 85 Broad Street occupies
the site of New York's very first city hall, a 1642 tavern
(the Stadt Herbergh) on Pearl Street converted for the
purpose in 1653 by the good burghers of the original
Dutch colony. Renamed the Stadt Huys (City Hall), it
stood here until 1697.

In 1980, before the construction of 85 Broad, the
site was temporarily turned over to a team who undertook New York's first large-scale archaeological dig.
Although they found no trace of the Stadt Huys, the
excavators did uncover the foundations of another
early building — the Lovelace Tavern, built in 1670 —
along with thousands of fragments of old Dutch
tobacco pipes, pieces of glass, and ceramic pottery
shards.

*Heritage Trails Site
Marker #G8: At
Pearl Street and
Coenties Slip, near
85 Broad Street*

Trinity Church and Graveyard, after 1933.

Wall Street and the Financial District

The buildings erected by or for the banks and brokerage houses that embody America's financial and economic heritage line Wall Street and the narrow, irregular streets nearby. This walk includes many of the most significant structures in the Financial District. The buildings that you will see are indicative of the great variety of structures erected for commercial uses in Lower Manhattan, such as the imposing Greek Revival style U.S. Custom House, completed in the 1840s; the dynamic New York Stock Exchange headquarters designed in 1901; and the enormous tower of the Manhattan Company, erected in 1929-30 and intended to be the world's tallest building. The tour also examines the history of some of the country's most significant financial enterprises — the Bankers Trust Company, the Manhattan Company, J. P. Morgan & Company, Brown Brothers Harriman, the Trust Company of America, the Bank of New York, and other firms that contributed to New York's preeminent position as a business and financial center. The varied scale of the buildings illustrates changes in technology that permitted the construction of soaring skyscrapers, but also reflects the symbolic value that some businesses placed on height and that others placed on their ability to maintain a modest building on a plot of land of enormous value.

Start: Trinity Church, Broadway at Wall Street.

⊕ WS1 Trinity Church and Graveyard

Broadway at Wall Street (Richard Upjohn, 1839-46). Standing imperiously at the head of Wall Street, Trinity Church is the financial district's most prominent religious institution. King William III of England granted the church a charter and some land in 1697, and the next year a church building was opened. At the time Trinity's third church was designed in 1839 (the first church burned, and the second suffered from structural problems), the congregation was one of the most influ-

81

ential in America, and its new building established the medieval-inspired Gothic Revival as the most appropriate style for churches. In order to create the illusion of a medieval English parish church, Richard Upjohn subtly employed brownstone blocks of varied hues, instantly lending the building a feeling of age and wear. The church is entered through a trio of bronze doors donated in 1896 as a memorial to John Jacob Astor II. The interior retains many of its original features, including plaster columns and ribs that are painted in imitation of stone and an 1844 chancel window designed by Upjohn. The churchyard, a beautiful green oasis amid Lower Manhattan's skyscrapers, contains many colonial-era stones, as well as memorials to Alexander Hamilton, Robert Fulton (his memorial bears a bronze diagram of his steamboat, the Clermont), Albert Gallatin (Jefferson's Secretary of the Treasury), Francis Lewis (signer of the Declaration of Independence), and William Bradford (printer and exponent of freedom of the press).

Leave the church-yard and go down the stairs into the Wall Street subway station.

WS2 Wall Street Subway Station

(Heins & La Farge, 1902-08). Even before the original Interborough Rapid Transit Company (IRT) subway opened its line running north from City Hall in 1904, an extension was underway into Lower Manhattan (WS2) and Brooklyn. The construction of the subway reflected the progressive spirit and importance of New York City, and the stations were designed as major architectural monuments. Wall Street's station was one of the most beautiful. Of particular interest are the colorful tile plaques illustrating the wooden wall and the stepped gable of a Dutch house, created by the Rookwood Pottery of Cincinnati, one of America's leading art-pottery firms.

Return to the street and stand on Broadway, opposite the foot of Wall Street.

WS3 Irving Trust Company Building

Now Bank of New York Building, 1 Wall Street, southeast corner Broadway (Voorhees, Gmelin & Walker; Ralph Walker, architect-in-charge, 1928-31). The Irving Bank was founded in 1851. It was named for Washington Irving, early-19th-century America's leading man of letters, in the hope that his name and likeness on the bank's notes would lend an air of quality to the new venture. During the 20th century the Irving developed strong correspondent relationships with foreign banks, becoming a leader in international banking. Befitting its prestige as one of New York's preeminent banks, the Irving Trust Company announced in May 1928 that it had purchased the plot at the corner of Broadway and Wall Street in one of the most expensive real estate transactions ever. The bank also purchased one of the world's preeminent addresses — 1 Wall Street. Appropriately, Irving Trust erected a masterpiece of skyscraper design (see drawing, p.28). The dynamic limestone-clad tower rises through a series of cliff-like setbacks to a crystalline crown. Architect Ralph Walker suggested that the gently undulating facades that resemble fabric gave new meaning to the term "curtain wall." The building not only was a symbol of the importance of Irving Trust, but was planned as a profitable investment, with 75 percent of the space available for rent. Irving intentionally sought a modern style for its new banking tower, providing a contrast to such contemporaneous bank buildings as the Bank of New York's far more conservative Colonial-inspired tower at 48 Wall Street (WS11). Ironically, Irving was taken over by the Bank of New York in 1988, and this great building is now its headquarters.

Unlike the Bank of New York Building, which has an interior ornamented with historical murals, Irving has a reception room (entered from Wall Street) that is among the most innovative spaces of the era. The multi-faceted bowed walls and ceiling are clad almost entirely in richly-colored glass mosaics that grade upward from deep red to orange, with an increasingly intense web of gold. The glass tesserae vary in color, shape, and texture, and even the mortar changes color, from dark blue on the walls to black on the ceiling. Custom-designed bronze tracery, radiator grilles, and lamps sparkle against the mosaics. The mosaic surfaces, which one critic compared to "free-hanging fabric," were designed by Walker in consultation with Hildreth Meière, who

Walk down Wall
Street and cross
Broad Street.
Stand on the
southeast corner.
The next four
entries are visible
from here.

served as a color consultant. Equally dramatic was the
observation lounge on the 49th floor, with its giant
windows through which light reflected off of a faceted
ceiling covered in silvery Philippine kappa shells.

WS4 Bankers Trust Company Building

14 Wall Street, northwest corner Nassau Street (Trowbridge & Livingston, 1910-12; addition, Shreve, Lamb &
Harmon, 1931-33). Bankers Trust was formed in 1903
by J.P. Morgan and other influential bankers in order to
provide trust services for commercial banks, a lucrative
service that these banks were forbidden by law to offer.
In order to retain customers whose business might be
lost to independent trust companies, the commercial
banks established their own trust company, which handled investment funds for estates, insurance companies,
and pension funds. Because it was closely allied with the
city's financial powerhouses, Bankers Trust was identi-
fied as one of the small "inner group" of banks controlling money and credit in the so-called "Money Trust"
investigation of 1913. After the Federal Reserve Act of
1914 allowed commercial banks to pursue trust banking, Bankers Trust branched out into commercial and
retail banking. It now offers a broad range of financial
and investment services from its Midtown headquarters
and its branches around the world. In 1999 Frankfurt-
based Deutsche Bank acquired Bankers Trust; the combined company is one of the world's largest banking
corporations.

The wealth and power of this bank are exemplified
by its purchase of an earlier skyscraper on the corner of
Wall and Nassau streets in what was the world's most
expensive recorded real-estate transaction. The Bankers
Trust Company Building exemplifies the balance
between a skyscraper erected as a symbol and advertise-
ment for its corporate sponsor and a commercial building that would generate substantial income for its owners. Bankers Trust commissioned a building that is
conservative in its use of Classical Greek motifs on the
exterior, but was innovative in its transformation of the
office building into a corporate landmark. The bank

84

Broad Street looking north to Bankers Trust Tower with New York Stock Exchange (left),
Equitable Building (rear), and Broad-Exchange Building (right), 1924.

became associated with the phrase "Tower of Strength," and the stepped pyramid atop the tower (housing mechanical equipment and storage rooms) became Bankers Trust's logo. The building is clad entirely in costly granite, cut by twelve hundred men at four different New England quarries; over 150,000 cubic feet of the stone was used. The monumental Ionic columns set above the rusticated base mark the location of the main banking hall and are balanced by a second colonnade near the roof. The bank expanded rapidly in the 1920s, and an L-shaped addition was commissioned from the architect of the Empire State Building. The exterior was planned to be subordinate to the original building. The project entailed the total redesign of the public banking hall. Much of the warm and inviting 1930s interior, paneled in Oregon myrtle burl and walnut, is extant, but its future is uncertain!

Wall Street looking east in 1923 with, from left to right, U.S. Custom House (Federal Hall), U.S. Assay Office, Merchant's Exchange (National City Bank), and J.P. Morgan & Co.

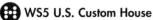

WS5 U.S. Custom House

Later U.S. Sub-Treasury, now Federal Hall National
Memorial, 26 Wall Street, northeast corner Nassau Street
(Town & Davis, Samuel Thompson, William Ross, and
John Frazee, 1833-42). In 1699, the colonial government erected a city hall on this site, which Major Pierre
Charles L'Enfant converted into Federal Hall (1788-89),
the nation's first capitol and the site where George
Washington took the presidential oath of office on April
30, 1789. This explains the name of the national memorial and the presence of John Quincy Adams Ward's
statue of Washington. The present building was erected
as the U.S. Custom House and, as such, became a center
of the federal government's financial activities. Duties
on goods landed at the Port of New York were paid in
the building's large rotunda. By 1861 more than $230
million in imported goods were cleared through the
Custom House each year.

Ithiel Town and Alexander Jackson Davis designed an
impressive Greek Revival style structure modeled on the
Parthenon. Although their design was altered somewhat
during construction, the building has always been con-
sidered one of the masterpieces of federal architecture
from the first half of the 19th century. A steep flight of
stairs (from which there is a superb view of surrounding
buildings) leads through the Doric colonnade into the
building, which contains a magnificent rotunda, probably the work of John Frazee, with shallow dome, monumental Corinthian columns, and beautiful iron railings
with figures that are half acanthus leaf and half bare-
breasted maiden.

After the Custom House moved to 55 Wall Street
(WS12) in 1862, the building was home to the U.S.
Sub-treasury. The New York arm of the Treasury was the
largest and most important — more than half the federal
government's money dealings were done through it.
Revenues due the federal government flowed in: duties
collected at the Custom House, receipts from post
offices, revenue deposits from national banks, income
from the sale of government bonds, and so on. Likewise,
interest payments to bond holders, pension payments,

and other government obligations were paid from the New York Sub-treasury. This ebb and flow of funds, "resembling those of an enormous bank," according to one observer, exceeded $2.5 billion a year at the end of the 19th century. In its basement vaults it kept reserves of cash and gold exceeding $200 million in value. The functions of the Sub-treasury were assumed by the Federal Reserve system, created in 1913. The building is now a museum run by the National Park Service.

⊞ WS6 J.P. Morgan & Company Building

23 Wall Street, southeast corner Broad Street (Trowbridge & Livingston, 1913-14). No name signifies financial power more than Morgan. The elder J. Pierpont Morgan went into business on this corner in 1873 in the firm of Drexel, Morgan & Co. In 1895, following Anthony Drexel's death, the firm was renamed J. P. Morgan & Company. Having long occupied an obsolete building on this site, in 1912 J.P. Morgan & Co. decided to move across the street and lease the top floor of the Bankers Trust Building (WS4). But the move never took place. The following year, the House of Representatives undertook its "Money Trust" investigation, which included an examination of Morgan's close relationship to several large New York banks, including Bankers Trust, and the company decided that the intended move would not be expedient. Instead, Morgan hired the same architectural firm as Bankers Trust and erected a new building constructed of three-foot-thick blocks of white Tennessee marble. At a time when enormous skyscrapers like the Bankers Trust Building were rising on surrounding plots, Morgan chose to erect a modestly-scaled structure on this extraordinarily valuable corner site, a move that subtly underlined the power of a financial institution that could afford a building that provided no income. Look carefully at the pockmarks on the Wall Street facade. They were made on September 16, 1920, when just before noon a horse-drawn wagon pulled up to the curb and moments later exploded, sending shrapnel flying in all directions. The blast killed 30 people and injured a hundred more. The Morgan banking floor was

J.P. Morgan

The legendary financial titan John Pierpont Morgan, though reviled
in the popular mind as a robber baron, was generally a stabilizing
influence in the cutthroat business environment of the Gilded Age.
Morgan shunned wasteful competition in industry, preferring to boost
profits through cooperation and consolidation. He was largely responsible for recapitalizing the railroad industry at the end of the 19th century
— reorganizing the Southern Railroad, the Erie Railroad, and the
Northern Pacific, among others — and he orchestrated the merger of
several enormous industrial corporations, including United States Steel,
the first corporation capitalized at $1 billion. Morgan's success made his
firm one of the world's most powerful banking houses, and he personally
came to symbolize wealth and power. A 1913 government investigation
of Morgan's influence in industry and finance found that he directly or
indirectly controlled or influenced 34 banks, 10 insurance companies,
32 railroads, 24 manufacturing corporations, and 12 public utilities—112 companies in all, worth about $22 billion. Morgan himself
denied any sinister notion of personal or financial control, claiming that
instead of wealth, connections, or even intellect, what really mattered in
business was character.

seriously damaged, and windows were shattered throughout the financial district. The press accused Bolsheviks and foreign anarchists of the act, but the actual perpetrator was never discovered. Pointedly, Morgan never repaired the scars.

Aftermath of the bomb explosion outside J.P. Morgan & Co., September 16, 1920.

WS7 New York Stock Exchange

8-18 Broad Street (George B. Post, 1901-03). The New York Stock Exchange is the world's largest and most widely-watched securities exchange. The NYSE's 1,366 members meet daily on its trading floor to buy and sell the stocks of over three thousand companies from around the globe, racking up volume of around one billion shares on an average day. The NYSE's origins stretch back to 1792, when 24 merchants and brokers met beneath a buttonwood tree to sign a compact pledging to trade with one another and charge a standard

commission fee to their customers. Stock trading
remained virtually unorganized, however, until 1817,
when a written constitution was adopted, formally
establishing the New York Stock Exchange. At that time
there were about 30 securities available for trading:
bonds issued by the federal government and the stocks
of local banks and insurance companies. The new
exchange rented rooms at 40 Wall Street and subsequently leased space in various downtown locations
until it purchased land and opened its own building at
this site in 1865 (enlarged in 1880-81). That building
was demolished in 1901 to make way for the present
white marble structure. The giant Classical Roman
Corinthian portico stands in front of the exchange's
famous trading hall. The pediment sculpture, *Integrity
Protecting the Works of Man*, was designed by John Quincy
Adams Ward and carved by Paul Wayland Bartlett.

*New York Stock
Exchange trading floor
set up for dedication
ceremonies, April 22,
1903.*

Hugh Ferris's roman-
tic charcoal drawing
for Manhattan Com-
pany Building,
c.1929.

WS8 U.S. Assay Office

Now New York Sports Club, 30 Wall Street (York & Sawyer, 1919-21; extension, Halsey, McCormack & Helmer, 1953-55). The United States Assay Office opened on this spot in 1853 in an elegant two-story building that originally housed a branch of the Second Bank of the United States (its facade is now preserved in the Metropolitan Museum of Art's American Wing). The assay office accepted deposits of gold or silver — in the form of nuggets, bullion, coin, or jewelry — determined the exact weight, grade, and value of the metals, and returned to the depositors their worth in coin or stamped bar. In 1919 the U.S. government commissioned a new assay office, now the lower three stories of this building. It is an elegant example of the work of York & Sawyer, America's preeminent early-20th-century bank designers, also responsible for the nearby Federal Reserve Bank (NW29). The building is an adaptation of the 17th-century urban palaces of Italy. Note the iron window guards with figures modeled after those on Michelangelo's Medici tombs.

Return to Wall Street and turn right.

WS9 Manhattan Company Building

Now Trump Building at 40 Wall Street, 40 Wall Street (H. Craig Severance; Yasuo Matsui, associate architect; Shreve & Lamb, consulting architect, 1929-30). This enormous 927-foot-tall, 71-story skyscraper was erected in an unprecedented twelve months beginning in May 1929. Credit for this feat is due to the building firm of Starrett Brothers & Eken, which was responsible for the construction of several of New York's tallest buildings, including this structure and the Empire State Building. Often toiling in three shifts, 24-hours a day, workers had the steel frame completed by November 1929 and worked simultaneously on the masonry cladding (one floor per day) and the interiors. W. Parker Chase, author of *New York The Wonder City*, a 1932 paean to New York, enthused: "No building ever constructed more thoroughly typifies the American spirit of hustle than does this extraordinary structure — *built in less than one year.*" The Manhattan Company's tower,

Continue down Wall Street.

with its stylized Classical base and Gothic spire, was the second tallest in the world at the time of its completion (the Chrysler Buildling in Midtown Manhattan was taller), and it remains a prominent presence on the Lower Manhattan skyline.

The early history of the Manhattan Company is connected with providing New York City with fresh water. In 1798 the city suffered through its worst yellow fever epidemic, which many physicians blamed on a fouled water supply. The next year, the Manhattan Company was founded to build a system that would deliver "pure and wholesome" water to municipal residents. The organization of the company was a rare common undertaking by political enemies Aaron Burr and Alexander Hamilton. Its charter included a clause enabling the company to use its excess capital for banking or "other monied transactions." Almost immediately the company opened an "office of discount and deposit," offering serious competition to Hamilton's Bank of New York. Successful in banking, the company was a failure at water: it sold its waterworks to the city in 1808. Thereafter the Bank of the Manhattan Company developed a strong commercial and retail banking network, finally merging with Chase National Bank in 1955 to become what is known today as Chase Manhattan Bank.

WS10 Trust Company of America Building
37 Wall Street (Francis H. Kimball, 1906-07). By the time that you take this tour, this building may be gone, because it stands on a portion of the site chosen for the construction of a new headquarters for the New York Stock Exchange. At the time of its completion, this dynamic Beaux-Arts style skyscraper designed by the ever versatile Francis H. Kimball (see p. 120) towered over neighboring structures. However, the placement of this slab-shaped building on a relatively narrow mid-block site indicates the pitfalls of constructing tall buildings on Lower Manhattan's narrow streets. The building was soon hemmed in on all sides, with few offices receiving natural light and air. The original tenant in the building was the Trust Company of America, one of the

Marble lower stories of the Trust Company of America Building, c.1907.

distressed banks rescued by J. P. Morgan during the panic of 1907. The panic was sparked on October 22 by a run on the Knickerbocker Trust Company. Nervous depositors demanded their funds from other banks, too, and by the close of business the following day, the Trust Company of America feared it would have to suspend operations. A consortium of big bankers led by Morgan bailed out this and other troubled banks with a multi-million-dollar rescue package. This was the last time a single individual could marshal so much financial power. The positive outcome of the panic was a clear indication of the need for a central banking system; it spurred development of the Federal Reserve System a few years later.

Walk to the corner of William Street.

WS11 Bank of New York and Trust Company Building

48 Wall Street, northeast corner William Street (Benjamin Wistar Morris, 1927-29). New York's first bank was founded in 1784, just three months after British troops ended their Revolutionary War occupation of the city. The Bank of New York was capitalized with $500,000 in silver and gold specie, giving it considerable stability in uncertain economic times. Alexander Hamilton was the bank's chief organizer: he drafted its constitution (at the age of 27) and was a director for the rest of his life. The bank settled at the corner of Wall and

William streets in 1797. The site served as its headquarters for two hundred years, until the present building was sold in 1998.

For its 1927 skyscraper headquarters, the Bank of New York chose a conservative design that combined the setbacks and tower form required by the city's zoning laws (see p. 125) with traditional Colonial-

Banking hall at the Bank of New York, c.1929.

inspired detail. This is evident at the pedimented entrance, the urns at the setbacks, the elegant cupola crowned by a republican eagle, and the Neoclassical second-floor banking hall embellished with historical murals painted by J. Monroe Hewlett. Two 18th-century relics are preserved in the building's facade: the 1797 cornerstone from the bank's original building on this parcel and a tablet commemorating the Bank of the United States, which opened the same year on the eastern portion of the site.

Continue a few yards east on Wall Street.

WS12 Merchants' Exchange

Later U.S. Custom House, then National City Bank, now Regent Wall Street Hotel, 55 Wall Street, between William and Hanover streets (Isaiah Rogers, 1836-42; addition, McKim, Mead & White, 1907-08). The Greek Revival Merchants' Exchange was one of the great building projects in early-19th-century New York, and the completed building, with its long row of Ionic columns and its shallow dome, was one of the city's most visible landmarks. The building replaced the first Merchants' Exchange, which opened in 1827 and burned in the Great Fire of 1835 (see p.99). The Exchange succeeded Wall Street's taverns and coffeehouses as a central meeting place where merchants, auctioneers, and brokers exchanged news and traded commercial goods. Its rotunda could accommodate three thousand merchants buying and selling all types of goods and merchandise. New York Stock Exchange brokers met in an upstairs room, while another section of the building was cordoned off for the "New Board of Stock Brokers," a rival stock exchange. The building also provided a home for the post office, offices of many brokers and insurance companies, facilities for a bank-note printer, and even a reading room that carried domestic and foreign newspapers.

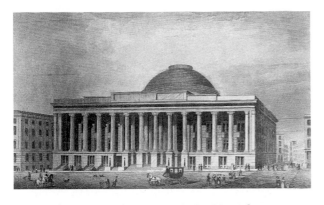

Merchants' Exchange, 1837.

After struggling to maintain the building for two decades, the stockholders finally sold it in 1862 to the U.S. Customs Service, which had outgrown its earlier building on Wall Street (WS5). In 1899, with the Customs Service set to build a new home on Bowling Green (BB9), the Exchange was purchased at public auction by National City Bank, the country's largest bank and one of the city's oldest merchant banks, established in 1812 (since 1976 it has been known as Citibank). The bank's president, James Stillman, realized that this beloved remnant of old New York, located on one of the most

McKim, Mead & White's monumental banking hall for National City Bank, c.1908.

prestigious Wall Street blocks, would be a fitting head-quarters site. However, the old Exchange was too small for the bank's needs and McKim, Mead & White was commissioned to design an addition, entailing the construction of a second colonnade faced with the same Quincy, Massachusetts, granite employed on the original. The interiors were gutted and replaced by the city's largest banking hall (measuring 188 by 124 feet), which, after standing vacant for many years when Citibank moved to new headquarters, is now in use as a small luxury hotel.

WS13 J.P. Morgan & Company Building
60 Wall Street (Kevin Roche, John Dinkeloo & Associates, 1984-89). Kevin Roche designed this mammoth office building as a late-20th-century variation on the early-20th-century Bankers Trust Building (WS4; if you look back, you will have an excellent view of the

stepped pyramid atop that building), with columnar base, unornamented shaft, columnar capital, and pyramidal rooftop. The enormous area of each floor reflects the demand of modern office tenants. In earlier buildings, tenants were confined to areas close to windows, necessary for light and ventilation. The invention of air conditioning and fluorescent lighting permitted efficient use of space far from windows, making buildings as large as this one efficient for office uses and economically appealing to realtors and investors who could rent every inch of space at maximum value.

Near the eastern end of this building stood the buttonwood tree beneath which, tradition holds, the New York Stock Exchange was founded in 1792. Wall Street's sole survivor of rapacious tree-cutting during the Revolution, the tree was a meeting place and a local landmark until it toppled in a storm in 1865. The "lone sycamore" was poetically eulogized in the local press.

Continue down Wall Street to the corner of Hanover Street.

WS14 Wall & Hanover Building (Brown Brothers & Company)

Now Brown Brothers Harriman & Co., 63 Wall Street, southeast corner Hanover Street (Delano & Aldrich with Yasuo Matsui, 1928-29). The Brown Brothers' patriarch, Alexander Brown, immigrated from Ireland

The Great Fire of 1835

A large portion of Lower Manhattan was destroyed in a disastrous fire that broke out during the night of December 16, 1835, at the store of Comstock & Andrews, a fancy dry goods merchant on Pearl Street. With a strong gale blowing on one of the coldest nights of the year, the fire quickly spread to adjacent buildings. Volunteer firemen pumped water from the East River, but their hoses froze in the subzero weather. By 1:00 a.m. the fire had reached the Merchants Exchange on Wall Street; its dome crashed down about three hours later. The fire engulfed 13 acres east of Broad Street and south of Wall Street. All told, it destroyed nearly 700 buildings—homes to the city's principal importers, exporters, and dry goods concerns worth about $16 million. The fire had several lasting effects. The burned district was rapidly rebuilt with what a contemporary eyewitness described as "acres of splendid granite, marble, brown stone and brick stores" (some of which survive and are on these tours). Nearly all the city's fire insurance companies were bankrupted by the disaster, forcing the industry to devise new methods of managing insurance risks. Finally, the fire confirmed the city's need for an abundant, reliable water supply. Construction of the Croton Aqueduct began shortly thereafter.

to Baltimore in 1800, set up a business importing Irish linen, and soon branched out into international banking. His four sons set up branch offices of the firm in other cities; James Brown established the New York City office in 1825. The firm was an important merchant bank, providing credit and foreign exchange to merchants, and was an early underwriter of securities issues. It specialized in guaranteed bills of exchange that allowed exporters to receive timely payment for their goods. Following the Banking Act of 1933, the firm remained a commercial bank, taking deposits and providing services mostly to large corporate clients. Brown Brothers & Company merged in 1931 with W. Averell Harriman's interests (BB16), forming Brown Brothers Harriman & Company. It remains one of a handful of surviving private banks.

Brown Brothers has been located at the corner of Wall and William streets since 1833. In 1928 the bank sold its modest headquarters building to a syndicate led by Starrett Brothers, Inc., a firm that also acted as the building contractor for the new skyscraper. The lower two stories and the basement were specifically designed for Brown Brothers and include a private corner entrance still used by the firm. The remaining 33 floors were planned for rental. Delano & Aldrich was one of the most prestigious architectural firms in New York

The Tontine Coffee House

The Tontine Coffee House, built on the northwest corner of Wall and Water streets in 1793 for the "common convenience ... of the mercantile community," was the center of New York commerce and society at the end of the 18th century. The Chamber of Commerce held its meetings there and the New York Stock Exchange brokers abandoned their buttonwood tree for the comforts of the Tontine. An English traveler described it in 1794: "The Tontine Tavern and Coffee House is a handsome large brick building; you ascend six or eight steps under a portico into a large public room, which is the Stock Exchange of New York where all bargains are made. The house was built to the accommodation of merchants. You can lodge and board there at a common table, and you pay ten shillings currency a day whether you dine out or not." Barrels, casks, and bundles were piled high on the sidewalks outside the Tontine as the merchants auctioned goods recently landed in the port. After a few decades, the commercial functions of the Tontine Coffee House were assumed by the Merchants' Exchange. The Tontine was razed in 1855, though the present office building on the site preserves the name.

City. Although this is the firm's only known skyscraper, it is a sophisticated work with setbacks and a light court that complied with the zoning laws (see p. 125), provided optimal space to tenants, and created a dynamically-massed structure clad in modest Neoclassical detail, the style favored by Delano & Aldrich. It is probable that the massing was the work of Yasuo Matsui, a Japanese-born and MIT-trained architect who was associated with the design of several of the most important skyscrapers of the 1920s, including this building and the Manhattan Company Building (WS9). Above the third floor, the building is ornamented with copies of ancient coins; coins were a popular decorative motif on bank buildings erected in Lower Manhattan in the 1920s. The building rose in only ten months, which was, according to the rental agents, one of the "speediest construction jobs on record."

Turn right on Hanover Street and walk to Exchange Place.

⊛ WS15 City Bank-Farmers Trust Company Building

20 Exchange Place (Cross & Cross, 1930-31). "One of the sights of New York," exclaimed *New York The Wonder City* in 1932, "Everything in connection with this monumental building expresses beauty, completeness and grandeur....[It] is the very last word in all that spells DELUXE." Indeed, this is one of the great overlooked buildings of New York, an impressive tower soaring above the narrow streets of the Financial District, combining representational ornamental detail with a lavish and often innovative use of materials. This was a difficult building to design since the architect had to take into consideration the sloping, oddly-shaped site (a snub-nosed triangle), the requirements of the city's zoning law (see p. 125), the spatial needs of two banks (City Bank-Farmers Trust and the Canadian Bank of Commerce), the desire to maximize profits from rental office space, and the requirements for substantial elevator service to accommodate the approximately seven thousand people who would occupy the building if fully rented.

The limestone-and-granite base of the building hugs the lot line, and at the first setback it is capped by four-

The "Giants of Finance" on the City Bank-Farmers Trust Company Building, with the Bank of New York Building at left.

teen colossal heads, the "Giants of Finance," seven scowling and seven grinning. These heads accent the main setback required by zoning, visually support the tower above, and have the utilitarian purpose of hiding exhaust vents. Explore the building carefully by walking along Exchange Place and William Street; it is filled with wonderful details. Note, in particular, the coins (representing principal countries where the bank had offices) that surround the main entrance on Exchange Place; the lobby with its mosaics, marbles, and metalwork; the window grilles on William Street embellished with figures representing professions such as agriculture, engineering, and architecture (a woman cradling a model of the building); and the doors at the corner of Exchange Place and William Street, which originally led into the City Bank-Farmers Trust Company offices. The doors exhibit early means of land, air, and water transport and their modern (c. 1930) equivalents, as well as symbols of industry and thrift. Like much of the other ornament on the building, the doors are cast from nickel silver, an alloy of nickel, zinc, and copper used here for the first time.

City Bank-Farmers' Trust was the nation's first trust company, founded in 1822 as the Farmers' Fire Insurance and Loan Company. Early on, the company wrote fire and life insurance policies and made agricultural loans, but it soon focused on trust management, investing securities and other assets on behalf of its clients. The company developed a large clientele of wealthy citizens and large corporations. In a 1929 merger, Farmers' became the trust affiliate of the National City Bank (WS12).

WS16 New York Cotton Exchange Building

60 Beaver Street, southeast corner William Street (Donn Barber, 1921-23). The eccentricity of New York's colonial street pattern has created a crossroads where five corners meet. The four surviving buildings form one of Lower Manhattan's finest architectural ensembles, with each building adapting to an oddly shaped site. The most conservative of the buildings is the Classical Revival style Cotton Exchange, a symbol of the importance of the cotton trade in generating wealth in the city. Established in 1870, the New York Cotton Exchange traded futures contracts — agreements to purchase or sell at a specified price a quantity of cotton that would be delivered at a future date. Futures trading helped growers market their crops before harvest and presented brokers with the opportunity to make a profit (or loss) on the fluctuating price of the commodity. The brokers gathered within a circular railing on the Exchange floor (located at the top of the building) and, as one observer noted, the trading was frenetic: "Brokers swarm in the 'pit' and all simultaneously make their offers to buy or sell....A word, a nod, a snap of the fingers and a contract is made." The minimum amount of a trade was 100 bales (50,000 pounds) of cotton. In 1976, after the Cotton Exchange had moved to the World Trade Center, its old building became one of the first downtown to be converted into apartments.

Walk down William Street to the crossroads of William Street, South William Street, and Beaver Street.

WS17 J.& W. Seligman & Company Building

Later Lehman Brothers, now Banca Commerciale Italiana, 1 William Street at South William Street (Francis H. Kimball with Julian C. Levi, 1906-07; alterations, Harry R. Allen, 1929; addition, Gino Valle, 1982-86). J. & W. Seligman & Company grew from a one-man retailing operation to become one of Wall Street's most prominent international banking houses. Its founder, Joseph Seligman emigrated from Germany in 1837 with $100 in his pocket and found work as a store clerk in a Pennsylvania mining town. A year later he quit to become a peddler. Over the next few years, his seven younger brothers joined him and the family business grew into a prosperous network of mercantile establishments, importing and retailing dry goods, clothing, and other merchandise in New York City, throughout the South, and westward to San Francisco. During the Civil War, Seligman was an important financial backer of the Northern forces. Using family and business connections, the firm sold $200 million in bonds in Germany on behalf of the credit-impaired Union government. In 1864, the brothers decided to focus their business entirely on banking and established the firm J.& W. Seligman & Company in New York. For years afterward, the firm was the U.S. government's fiscal agent in Europe. After the Civil War, the firm increased its investment activities, underwriting railroad and corporate securities. It continues business as an investment advisor and manager of mutual funds.

As its space needs increased, the Seligman firm chose to erect its own prestigious bank building rather than invest in a large skyscraper with extensive rental space. Francis Kimball (see p. 120), in association with a Seligman relative, Julian Levi, designed a richly sculptural limestone building with a crowning tempietto (a round temple) that is the focal point of the building. When the Seligman bank relocated in 1919, Lehman Brothers, another legendary investment firm established by German-Jewish immigrants, purchased the building. In an alteration, the main entrance was moved from South William Street to the curved corner. Samuel Yellin (see

p. 142) crafted the beautiful iron doors. In 1980
Lehman Brothers left the building, selling it to Banca
Commerciale Italiana. Italian architect Gino Valle's addi-
tion is a handsome modern abstraction of Kimball and
Levi's original design, including, at the corner of Stone
Street and Mill Lane, a metal tower that echoes the origi-
nal tempietto.

WS18 Delmonico's

56 Beaver Street at William Street (James Brown Lord,
1890-91). Swiss immigrants John and Peter Delmonico
introduced fine Continental cuisine to New Yorkers at
their famous restaurant, founded in 1827. Joined by
their nephew Lorenzo, their restaurant became world
famous for elegant, leisurely meals enjoyed by society's
elite. The menu in 1838 ran 11 pages long and featured
47 kinds of veal, 50 fish dishes, and 21 different Bor-
deaux wines. Delmonico's introduced salads to the
American palate and invented several noted dishes,
including lobster Newburg and baked Alaska. The
restaurant moved several times, following its clientele
uptown, but in 1891 reopened a branch in this building
that catered to the Wall Street lunch crowd. The Renaissance Revival restaurant and office building replaced a
smaller restaurant on the site. The coloration of the
materials — the light brown of the Belleville, New Jersey, sandstone base; the deep orange of the brick; and
the matching terra-cotta ornament — is especially note-
worthy. Beneath the entrance portico is a pair of marble
columns, reputed to be from ancient Pompeii, that had
graced the entrance to the earlier restaurant.

Walk down
William Street to
Hanover Square.

⦿ WS19 Hanover Bank

Now India House, 1 Hanover Square (1851-54). This
brownstone building is the only surviving example of
the Italianate style commercial palazzi erected by New
York's leading banks in the 1850s as their businesses
rapidly expanded with the booming American economy. The building was the first office of the Hanover
Bank, established in 1851 with $500,000 in capital.
Its commercial banking business prospered, and over

the years it built a strong nationwide network of correspondent banks. In a 1961 merger it became Manufacturers Hanover Trust (which has since merged into Chase Manhattan Bank). The bank remained here until about 1870. Subsequently, the building housed the New York Cotton Exchange (WS16) and the shipping firm W. R. Grace and Company. Since 1921 it has been India House, a private luncheon club founded in 1918 by diplomat and foreign financier Willard Straight and others. Its membership consisted mostly of businessmen active in shipping and international trade. The club's name derives from "India" and "the Indies," which were words that connoted the exotic in world trade. The club owns an impressive collection of maritime art. The public may dine here too, at Harry's (downstairs) and Bayard's (upstairs).

Hanover Bank Building, c.1910.

WS20 First Precinct Police Station

Now New York City Landmarks Preservation Commission, 100 Old Slip (Hunt & Hunt, 1909-11). In 1845 New York's first professional police force was established. In addition to keeping a watchful eye on thieves, gamblers, and prostitutes, the police performed many civic and social service duties: cleaning streets, inspecting tenements, and providing shelter for the homeless. As the system expanded, custom-built precinct houses were erected throughout the city. The First Precinct's building is one of the most impressive. Modeled after a 15th-century Florentine palazzo, its bold design reflects the importance that the city placed on the design of even the smallest civic structures. The limestone building has a monumentality appropriate for a police station located in the commercial center of the city. In 1993 the building was converted into the offices of the Landmarks Preservation Commission, the city agency that designates landmarks and regulates buildings and districts of architectural, historical, and cultural importance, including many of the buildings on these tours.

Continue down William Street. Cross Pearl Street, the location of Manhattan's original shoreline, and Water Street.

Turn left on Water Street.

WS21 77 Water Street

(Emery Roth & Sons, 1968-70; Corchia, de Harak, Inc, designer; A.E. Bye Associates, landscape architect). The architecture of this office building is undistinguished, but the street-level design commissioned by the William Kaufman Organization provides a whimsical environment that includes a river with a school of fish, "lollipop" benches, a miniature candy store, and several pieces of sculpture.

Wall Street lives and dies on communications, from bicycle messengers, to subterranean systems of pneumatic tubes, to telephone and telegraph, to ticker-tape, to electronic readouts, to fax machines, and now, the Internet. And the revolution in communications technology is transforming how people work and live in Lower Manhattan. As always, New York is living up to its name by being open to the new.

This 1960's office building has been ripped apart and rewired with an unmatched 21st century communications infrastructure that can instantly connect its tenants with sites around the world. Famous in the 1980's as the high finance offices of investment bankers Drexel Burnham Lambert, 55 Broad Street has been reborn as the Downtown headquarters of Silicon Alley — the dazzlingly hip computer and new media industries stretching along Broadway from 23rd Street down through the financial district.

The new media, on-line services, and software companies relocating here are devoted to the proposition that communications technology eliminates the significance of time and distance — allowing us to do business with the world from a remote mountain top. Yet these very companies and the people who run them cluster here in the heart of Downtown for human warmth, commonality of interests, and deal-cementing, real-world handshakes — traditional Downtown values.

Heritage Trails Site Marker #G17: In front of 55 Broad Street, corner of Beaver Street

What more appropriate home for the Museum of American Financial History than the Standard Oil Building, formerly the home of the world's first modern international corporation, founded by the financial titan, John D. Rockefeller? Rising above Bowling Green, following the curve at the foot of Broadway, it is one of Downtown's most dramatic skyscrapers, a great Renaissance palace topped by a classical urn that emitted smoke from burning oil, proclaiming the power and wealth of the industry housed within this landmark.

Over two centuries ago, this was the site of the young Alexander Hamilton's law office. As America's first Secretary of the Treasury, Hamilton laid the groundwork for today's economic system. In his private life, unfortunately, he was less successful. When he died at age 49, shot by Aaron Burr in a duel in New Jersey, Hamilton left his family penniless. One of the cherished documents in the Museum is a share in the Trust created by his many friends to support his widow and children.

This intimate Museum is the only one of its kind in America, displaying the actual stocks and bonds bought and sold on Wall Street, as well as other artifacts of securities industry history. Exhibits include rare examples of Colonial currency, railroad securities, a 100-dollar bond for the Republic of Texas issued in 1845, historic paintings and photographs of the financial district, and old stock tickers.

Heritage Trails Site Marker #G16:
In front of
28 Broadway,
across from "The
Bull" statue

Building the Brooklyn Bridge was the mission of a remarkable dynasty. Two generations of the Roebling family gave their all to see it through. John Augustus Roebling, wire-rope manufacturer and pioneer builder of suspension bridges, conceived of and tirelessly promoted the bridge; he was named its chief engineer at the onset of construction in 1867. He died two years later, after a freak accident at dockside. His son, Washington, also a gifted engineer and master builder, assumed his duties until he was felled by caisson disease and was confined to his Brooklyn Heights apartment. From his bedside, his wife Emily Warren Roebling took over and saw the project through for another decade to its triumphant completion.

The Brooklyn Bridge is the foremost engineering achievement of the 19th century. It was the world's longest suspension bridge, made possible by the use of the structural advance of braided iron cables. Supporting its enormous weight required masonry towers that were then the tallest, heaviest, and deepest structures on the North American continent. On opening day, May 25, 1883, over 150,000 people walked across the Brooklyn Bridge, higher above the East River than they had ever been.

Heritage Trails Site Marker #R8: Manhattan side of Bridge at entrance to pedestrian walkway

Many citizens of New York and Brooklyn hated the idea of the bridge, fearing it would only lead to merger of what then two separate cities, the country's first and third largest respectively. This did occur, in 1898, with the creation of the City of Greater New York. But the enduring beauty of the bridge has inspired tributes from poet Hart Crane, artist Frank Stella, historian Lewis Mumford, and scores of others — even an Italian chewing gum (Brooklyn — il gum de ponte). Take a walk across the Brooklyn Bridge. It's free, and it offers staggering views of the skyline, the harbor, and the soaring Gothic vaults of the bridge itself.

The Seamen's Church Institute is one of the city's oldest maritime establishments. Founded in 1834 to minister to merchant seafarers, in 1844 the Institute launched floating chapels — Gothic buildings on East River barges — for sailors wary of dry land. The chapels proved so unexpectedly popular with landlubbers that seats had to be reserved for the seafarers, testifying to New Yorker's love of novelty.

Though the floating chapels are long gone, the Institute today serves over 150,000 sailors from more than 75 nations from its Water Street building, which houses a permanent chapel and gallery. The Water Street Gallery, an indispensable part of the South Street Seaport's attractions, mounts exhibitions drawn from its enormous collection, which includes 18th century engravings, Currier & Ives prints, sextants, compasses, whaling tools, scrimshaw, watercolor tatoo designs, ships-in-a-bottle, and ship builder's scale models.

The Institute's award-winning new quarters deftly combine historic preservation and modern whimsy. The design, by architects James Stewart Polshek and Partners, suggests nothing so much as a steamship tied up at South Street Seaport. The architects restored a 1799 ships chandlery; modeled an extension on its brick, windows, and storefront; and then let their nautical imagination loose on the upper decks, using enameled metal panels, pipe railings, and a yardarm flying the Institute's colors.

Heritage Trails Site Marker #B5: Opposite 241 Water Street in the South Street Seaport Historic District

North of Wall Street: Counting-Houses to Skyscrapers

Beginning with St. Paul's Chapel, New York's most significant surviving Colonial-era building, this tour explores a section of Lower Manhattan with an extraordinary diversity of buildings — the modest warehouses or counting-houses of the early-nineteenth-century seaport city, pioneering late-nineteenth-century efforts at tall-building construction, great skyscrapers from almost every decade of the twentieth century, and modestly-scaled churches, banks, and other structures. There is no section of New York where the dynamic contrast between small-scale early commercial buildings and the monumental buildings of a great modern city is so clearly evident.

Start: St. Paul's Chapel, Broadway between Fulton and Vesey streets.

⦙⦙ NW1 St. Paul's Chapel

Broadway and Fulton Street (1764-66; porch, 1767-68; tower, James C. Lawrence, 1794). St. Paul's, a chapel of Trinity Church (WS1), is one of America's great colonial-era religious buildings. The design of the building is often misattributed to an architect named Thomas McBean, who is said to have studied with English master James Gibbs; however, there is no evidence that McBean ever existed. St. Paul's is, indeed, a simplified version of Gibbs's St. Martin-in-the-Fields, London, but this building was known to American builders through a book illustrating Gibbs's work. In place of the expensive stonework employed in London, St. Paul's is constructed of local Manhattan schist with brownstone trim. The brownstone portico on Broadway is actually the rear of the church. Beneath the portico is a dynamic funerary memorial commissioned by Congress in memory of Major General Richard Montgomery, who died during an attack on Quebec in 1775. While in Paris in 1777, Benjamin Franklin commissioned the monument from

French sculptor Jacques Caffieri. St. Paul's is one of the few churches that was not damaged during the Revolutionary War, and it was here that Lord Howe and the future King George IV (a navy midshipman) worshiped while the city was occupied, and here that George Washington prayed while New York served as the nation's first capital (his box pew is preserved in the north aisle).

Notable features of the vaulted interior are the Neoclassical funerary monuments, similar in style to those found in English parish churches; a "wine-glass" pulpit crowned with Prince of Wales feathers, thought to be the only British royal symbol in New York still in its original location; the exuberant French-inspired altar rail and Glory panel with the Ten Commandments, designed by French emigré architect Pierre L'Enfant several years before he planned Washington, D.C.; and the fourteen Irish Waterford chandeliers dating from about 1802. The front entrance to the church faces the graveyard where several beautifully carved 18th-century markers survive. Two granite monuments commemorate Irish patriots who were forced to flee Ireland and settled in New York (neither is actually buried here) — an obelisk commemorating Thomas Emmet (an Episcopalian), on the corner of Broadway and Fulton Street; and the pillar near Broadway and Vesey Street, in memory of William McNeven (a Roman Catholic), with inscriptions in English, Latin, and Gaelic.

NW2 American Telephone & Telegraph (AT&T) Company Building

Now Kalikow Building, 195 Broadway between Fulton and Dey streets (William Welles Bosworth, 1912-16, 1921-24). Little expense was spared in the construction of this headquarters building for AT&T, one of the world's largest corporations. The American Telephone & Telegraph Company was incorporated in 1885 to connect the many local telephone systems operated by the American Bell Telephone Company. Two years later it inaugurated the nation's first long-distance service, from New York City to Albany and Boston. By the turn of the

Leave St. Paul's Chapel and turn right on Broadway. Walk south to the corner of Fulton Street.

Evelyn Longman's "Genius of Electricity," popularly known as "Golden Boy," which once crowned the AT&T Tower, c. 1920.

century, practically all the large towns and cities east of Omaha and Kansas City were knit together in a nation-wide system. In 1899 AT&T took over the business of the Bell system, creating the monopoly that would ulti-mately centralize and coordinate all local and long-dis-tance telephone service in the United States under the guiding business tenet "One system, one policy, univer-sal service." A federal antitrust suit filed against the com-pany resulted in the 1984 breakup of the Bell system and in divestiture of the seven regional telephone compa-nies, bringing about greater competition in long-dis-tance telephone service.

The Greek-inspired exterior of the former AT&T headquarters, with its tiers of fluted columns — Doric at the base and Ionic above — is clad entirely in expensive white Vermont granite with solid bronze trim. The building was erected in two campaigns, beginning with the corner section on Broadway and Dey Street and the narrow extension extending to Fulton Street that includes the tower topped by a stepped pyramid once surmounted by a golden statue. As part of the second construction period, the four Broadway entrances were embellished with Paul Manship's bronze relief panels representing the four elements — Earth, Air, Fire, and Water.

Go into the lobby of the building, if it is open.

Suffused with a sense of calm and mystery, the lobby is one of the most unusual spaces in New York. It is composed of a forest of Italian marble columns, each constructed around a structural steel column, which create the feel of the interior of a Greek temple. The space is lit by Classical lanterns of bronze and translucent alabaster. Great care was taken in every detail. Above the bronze elevator doors are frolicking putti; those in the original wing are by Manship, but he was unavailable to continue the job, and Gaston Lachaise carved the somewhat chubbier putti in the addition. Also notice the marble mailbox at the rear of the south side of the lobby, modeled on an ancient altar; it was so unusual that special permission for its use had to be obtained from the Post Office Department in Washington. Chester Beach was responsible for the heroic male figure in the World War I memorial that faces the Broadway entrances.

NW3 Corbin Building

192 Broadway, northeast corner John Street (Francis H. Kimball, 1888-89). It may take a few minutes of looking to appreciate the beauty of this sadly neglected early skyscraper (it may not be tall by our standards, but in 1889 it was quite an impressive sight). This is an important work by Francis Kimball, who would go on to design some of the city's most prominent tall buildings (see p. 120). The lower three stories are clad in two types of

Walk south on Broadway to the southwest corner of Dey Street and look diagonally across to the northeast corner of Broadway and John Street.

sandstone, while the upper floors are a custom-made tawny-colored brick with cast-iron and reddish-brown terra-cotta ornament. If cleaned, the various materials would harmonize, just as Kimball intended. Kimball was a pioneer in the use of terra cotta (clay ornament made in molds and fired), and the exuberant window enframements, columns, and scalloped arches attest to his talents. Contemporary critics were amazed that the building was designed and built in only eleven months.

Cross Broadway to get a closer look at the Corbin Building and then walk south on Broadway to Maiden Lane.

⊞ NW4 Maiden Lane Jewelry District.

A stream once ran along the current route of Maiden Lane where, according to tradition, the young women of New Amsterdam gathered to wash the family linen, giving it the Dutch name, *Maagde Paetje* (Maiden's Path). Another tradition holds that amorous swains met the maidens there for other activities. By the middle of the 19th century, New York City's major industries had begun to concentrate in particular localities — banking on Wall Street, insurance on Pine Street, and jewelry and watches on Maiden Lane. By the 1870s, Maiden Lane was America's center for the manufacture and importation of jewelry, watches, and precious stones. These businesses were located in old buildings until the late 19th century, when a series of large new structures were erected, most of which are still standing, including the Jewelers' Building (Ralph S. Townsend, 1897) at No. 11; the Diamond Exchange (Gilbert A. Schellenger, 1893-94) at No. 14; and the Silversmiths' Building (Clinton & Russell, 1907-08) at No. 17. All of the jewelry businesses have left the area, many departing for West 47th Street in the 1920s, with the notable exception of William Barthman, on the northeast corner of Broadway and Maiden Lane. Barthman opened on Maiden Lane in 1884 and by the following year had moved to this corner location, relocating briefly while the present Cushman Building (C.P.H. Gilbert, 1897-98) was under construction. A most unusual feature is the clock, possibly dating from the 1920s, embedded in the sidewalk near the corner of the store.

Cross Broadway and walk west on Cortlandt Street to Church Street.

Maiden Lane looking east from Broadway with advertisements for jewelry and watch firms, c.1870.

NW5 East River Savings Bank

Now Century 21, 26 Cortlandt Street, northeast corner Church Street through to Dey Street (Walker & Gillette, 1933-34). Attorney John Leveridge founded the East River Savings Institution in his rowhouse at 145 Cherry Street on the Lower East Side in 1848. Savings banks aimed to encourage "provident habits" among the city's working class and were among the fastest-growing banks before the Civil War. By 1895, deposits at East River Savings had grown to more than $10 million. The bank had occupied several Lower Manhattan homes and had opened a branch office on the Upper West Side before settling here in 1935. Real estate observers were shocked when the bank announced that it would erect only a two-story building on a plot worth $3 million.

Banking hall of the
East River Savings
Bank, c.1935.

The headquarters building has a conservative exterior
faced in Alabama limestone, with polished gray Quincy,
Massachusetts, granite trim employed at the base,
around the doors, and for the stylized eagles sculpted by
Benjamin Hawkins. The bank welcomed its hard-work-
ing depositors into a vast light-filled space with richly-
textured walls of red, black, and gold marble and white
travertine, and an enormous mural by Dale Stetson
depicting the East River as it flows past Manhattan. Several years ago the banking hall was taken over by the discount emporium Century 21. Although the space is now
crammed with men's clothing, most of the original fea-

Walk to the corner
of Cortlandt and
Church streets.

tures are still evident (enter on Church Street or through
the store's main doors on Cortlandt Street).

118

 **NW6 World Trade Center**

Church Street between Liberty and Vesey streets
(Minoru Yamasaki, 1966-77). From Church Street you
can get an overview of the World Trade Center complex,
consisting of the two huge towers, a series of rather
banal low dark-glass structures, and a vast plaza.
Although the design of the complex has never been
very popular with New Yorkers, the twin towers have
become an iconic image of the city, and, on a clear day,
the view from the observatory can make even a jaded
New Yorker's jaw drop.

Walk south on
Church Street.
Turn left on Liberty
Street and stand in
Liberty Plaza.

NW7 1 Liberty Plaza and Liberty Plaza Park

Broadway and Church Street between Cortlandt,
Liberty, and Cedar streets (Skidmore, Owings & Merrill;
Roy Allen, Jr., architect-in-charge; 1969-74). This
brooding black steel building was erected by U.S. Steel
as its headquarters, but the firm chose not to occupy the
building. The enormous bulk and height were created
by transferring air rights from the block to the south,
which became a plaza. This rather bleak space has been
controversial since it opened. Two full blocks of historic
buildings were cleared for this project, including the
magnificent Singer Tower, which has the dubious distinction of being the tallest building ever demolished.

Walk to the north-
west corner of
Broadway and
Cedar Street. Look
at the vista down
Cedar Street to the
tower of the Cities
Service Building
(NW15) and the
slab of the Chase
Manhattan Bank
Building (NW12).

NW8 Marine Midland Building

Now HSBC, 140 Broadway between Liberty and Cedar
streets (Skidmore, Owings & Merrill; Gordon Bunshaft,
architect-in-charge; 1964-67). Gordon Bunshaft's elegantly minimalist trapezoidal building is one of the
great masterpieces of Modern skyscraper design. The
beautifully proportioned bands of bronze-colored glass
set flush with the black aluminum framing, resemble a
paper wrapping hiding the building's structure. This
building provides a vivid contrast with the same architect's nearby silvery Chase Manhattan Bank (NW12),
with its exposed framing. The drama of the irregularly-
shaped Marine Midland Building is heightened by
Isamu Noguchi's orange steel rhombohedron (an elon-
gated cube) punctured by an aluminum tunnel, which

is precariously balanced on the plaza along Broadway. Since the building's completion it has been the home of Marine Midland, a bank that was founded in 1850 in Buffalo to finance shipping along the Great Lakes. The bank later expanded across the "midlands" of the state, serving the important industrial and agricultural sections of western and northern New York. In 1987 Marine Midland became the principal U.S. subsidiary of HSBC Holdings plc, a London-based global banking company, and in 1998 adopted its parent's name, HSBC.

Cross to the southeast corner of Broadway and Cedar Street and look back across Broadway.

NW9a Trinity Building

111 Broadway, southwest corner Thames Street (Francis H. Kimball, 1904-05; addition along Thames Street, 1907) and **NW9b U.S. Realty Building**, 115 Broadway between Cedar and Thames streets (Francis H. Kimball, 1906-07). This pair of buildings exemplifies early-20th-century speculative skyscraper construction and attests to Francis Kimball's talent at designing striking skyscrapers that pleased developers as well as tenants. Each was erected on an extremely narrow site, with its interior spaces arranged in an efficient manner. Elevators rise along dark and narrow Thames Street so that profitable office space can occupy the Trinity Building's long,

---

Francis Hatch Kimball

Although not very well known today, Francis Kimball was one of the most talented architects active at the turn of the century, and he was a pioneer in the design and engineering of skyscrapers. Kimball established an office in New York in 1879 and was responsible for a wide variety of buildings, designed in many styles. He was among the first architects to employ decorative architectural terra cotta, as is evident at the beautiful Corbin Building (NW3), one of his earliest tall office buildings. Beginning in the 1890s, Kimball designed a succession of steel-skeleton-frame skyscrapers of enormous size — the Trinity (NW9a) and U.S. Realty (NW9b) buildings, the Adams Express Building (BB17a), the Empire Building (BB17c), and the Trust Company of America Building (WS10), among others — each of which rises to the maximum height that was economically viable for its site and contains no setbacks. As might be expected from one of the city's most successful skyscraper architects, Kimball was resolutely opposed to any zoning law that would regulate skyscraper construction, feeling that such regulation was unconstitutional and would permanently lower property values (neither of which turned out to be true).

Drawing of the Trinity and U.S. Realty Company Buildings, c. 1904.

light-filled elevation along Trinity Church's cemetery and the U.S. Realty Building's frontage along Cedar Street (there was no park on the north side of Cedar Street in 1907). Both buildings have steel skeleton frames supported on foundations sunk 85 feet below Broadway. Each is clad in Indiana limestone punctuated with pairs of windows that light individual offices. The facades are highlighted with a pastiche of Gothic-inspired pointed arches, buttresses, gargoyles, pinnacles, and other details that both relate to the style of nearby Trinity Church (WS1) and create handsome elevations that would be attractive to prospective tenants. Speculative building developers often invested money in lobby design, since the lobby created an image that was crucial for attracting prestigious tenants willing to pay high rents. These two extraordinary lobbies (recently restored) contain elaborate marble, bronze, iron, leaded-glass, and mosaic fittings.

The United States Realty & Construction Company, incorporated in 1902, was a leading real estate investment and management firm. It controlled several important real estate developers, including the George A. Fuller Company, owner of the Flatiron Building at 23rd Street and Broadway. Besides this building and the Trinity Building next door, it owned several properties in the financial district, including the Whitehall Building (BB6). It merged in 1946 with Sheraton Corporation. Until 1979 the Lawyer's Club, one of the oldest Wall Street luncheon clubs, was housed in elegantly appointed rooms on the top floors of the U.S. Realty Company Building.

Cross back to the west side of Broadway to visit the lobbies of the Trinity and U.S. Realty buildings and then walk south on Broadway, stopping opposite Pine Street.

NW10 American Surety Building

100 Broadway, southeast corner Pine Street (Bruce Price, 1894-96; addition, Herman Lee Meader, 1920-22). The American Surety Company was formed in 1881 and opened for business three years later at 160 Broadway. It dealt in surety bonds, a branch of insurance that guarantees that a person will perform an obligation. The most familiar example is a bail bond, which guarantees that a person released from jail will appear in

court. In addition to judicial bonds, American Surety offered fidelity bonds, which covered bank, brokerage, and government employees; fiduciary bonds for cases involving executors and administrators of estates and trusts; and commercial bonds guaranteeing faithful performance by contractors, shippers, and warehousemen. American Surety grew to be the biggest company in its field. By 1924 it had 15,000 local agents working at 40 branch offices across North America. It merged with Transamerica Corporation in 1963.

The building that the American Surety Company erected has generally been regarded as one of the most significant early skyscrapers. American Surety spent a great deal of money on this steel-framed building, cladding in granite all four elevations of what was once

Looking north up Broadway, the American Surety Company Building rises as a free-standing tower, 1898.

a tower visible from all sides (Price abhorred the blank side and rear walls of most tall buildings) and commissioning classically-garbed statues from sculptor J. Massey Rhind. The division of the two street facades into an ornate base, simple shaft, and decorative capital provided a precedent for the tripartite skyscraper, massed in a manner reminiscent of a classical column, that became popular in the early 20th century. The tower retained its freestanding character until four-bay-wide extensions, matching the original design, were added to both street elevations in 1920-22.

Look to the northeast (your left).

🎯 NW11 Equitable Building

120 Broadway (Ernest Graham & Associates; Peirce Anderson, architect-in-charge; 1913-15). The Equitable Life Assurance Society was founded by Henry Baldwin Hyde, an employee of the Mutual Life Insurance Company who struck out on his own in 1859, opening an office on the floor above his former employer. The company's early success was due in part to the backing it got from wealthy congregants of the Fifth Avenue Presbyterian Church and Hyde's aggressive sales campaigns, but the key to Equitable's growth was a new type of insurance policy — the tontine. Grouped together by age, tontine policyholders agreed to forgo dividend payments for an agreed term, say ten or twenty years. Relieved of the duty to pay dividends during the interim, the insurance company invested the premiums and built up a surplus fund. As policyholders died, their estates received only the face value of the insurance policy and their dividends were used to increase the share paid to the remaining living policyholders. The longer a person lived, the bigger the dividend grew, until the final survivor enjoyed the entire payout. Betting on one's own longevity gave the tontine policy a gambling allure that made the policies enormously popular and profitable. By 1899, the year of Hyde's death, sales of tontine policies had made Equitable the biggest insurance company in the world, with more than $1 billion of insurance in force. Tontine policies were banned in 1906, but Equitable continued to prosper. Today it is

From left to right, Trinity Building, Equitable Building, American Surety Building (with extension), and First National Bank Building (Walker & Gillette, 1932-33). The crowning pyramid to the Bankers Trust Building is at upper right.

Zoning

By the early twentieth century, architects, critics, and the general public were debating the issue of skyscraper regulation. As buildings rose to ever-taller heights, people began to fear that no light or air would ever reach the sidewalks along the narrow streets of Lower Manhattan. A plan to regulate the bulk, but not the height, of skyscrapers was developed and debated. The announcement of the plan to construct the massive Equitable Building (NW11) in 1913 spurred the debate, and in 1916 New York City passed America's first zoning law. The law stated that as skyscrapers rose, their bulk had to step back. Since no effort was made to cap the height of buildings, the law permitted the construction of a tower of any height rising on 25 percent of the area of a building lot. This accounts for the classic New York skyscraper profile — a bulky mass with a series of setbacks crowned by a slender tower — evident at four great skyscrapers in Lower Manhattan: the Irving Trust Company (WS3), the Manhattan Company (WS9), the City Bank-Farmers Trust Company (WS15), and the Cities Service (NW15) buildings. The 1916 zoning law remained in effect until 1961 when it was superseded by a new code favoring slab-shaped towers set in plazas, resulting in skyscrapers such as the Marine Midland Building (NW8) and Wall Street Plaza (NW16).

Isamu Noguchi's Chase Manhattan plaza fountain at night, 1964.

one of the nation's premier providers of life insurance and financial services.

In 1868-70, less than a decade after the firm had been founded, Equitable erected the world's first office building with an elevator, located on the corner of Broadway and Cedar Street. Many consider this building to be the world's first skyscraper. The building eventually expanded onto the entire block (see photograph, p. 20) before burning in a spectacular fire in 1912. Rather than finance a new building, Equitable sold this site to a syndicate headed by Thomas Coleman Du Pont, which erected this massive H-shaped speculative office building. At the time of its completion, this was the largest building in the world in terms of square footage of floor space, with 1,220,000 square feet of rental space. Equitable rented only three floors. The Chicago architecture firm hired to design the building was not asked to produce an architectural monument. Rather, the builders were interested in a technologically up-to-date structure that would generate a substantial income. The result was an efficient fireproof building with 48 elevators to serve the 16,000 office workers who would use the structure each day. The building was so mammoth that its construction spurred a concurrent campaign to create a zoning law prohibiting this type of structure, a campaign that was successful in 1916 (see p.125).

The building has a restrained Classical exterior. It is entered through a grand triumphal arch that leads into an impressive lobby modeled on an ancient Roman basilica. This was an appropriate image for an office building lobby, since Roman citizens met friends and undertook business in the basilicas of ancient forums.

 NW12 Chase Manhattan Bank and Plaza

1 Chase Manhattan Plaza (Skidmore, Owings & Merrill; Gordon Bunshaft, architect-in-charge; 1955-62). Chase National Bank was founded in 1877 and named for Salmon P. Chase, Secretary of the Treasury during the Civil War and architect of the national banking system, who had died four years earlier. In a one-room office at 117 Broadway, the bank took in deposits of $15,000

Walk through the Equitable Building lobby to Nassau Street. Cross Nassau Street and turn left. Turn right onto Chase Manhattan Plaza. If the lobby is closed, walk along Pine Street, turn left on Nassau Street, and enter Chase Manhattan Plaza.

on its first day of business. By the mid-20th century, Chase was a leader in correspondent, commercial, and international banking. It was the first U.S. bank to open branch offices in Germany and Japan following the close of World War II. In 1955 it merged with the Bank of the Manhattan Company (WS9), greatly strengthening its retail banking operations. David Rockefeller, grandson of John D., was chairman of the bank from 1969 to 1981 and raised Chase's profile in international finance even more. Several prominent banks have been folded into the Chase name in recent years, including Manufactures Hanover and Chemical Bank, making Chase Manhattan one of today's biggest global banking corporations.

Chase Manhattan's striking aluminum and glass building set on a large plaza is one of the preeminent International Style skyscrapers and one of the most influential buildings in the history of commercial development in Lower Manhattan. The building is a total break from the traditional masonry office buildings that surround the site, centralizing its floor area into a single slab with no setbacks, exploiting the transparency of glass and the sheen of the aluminum panels that cover its structural framework, and juxtaposing a huge tower and vast plaza. This was the first major new building in Lower Manhattan since the early 1930s, and at a time when many businesses were moving to Midtown, it rehabilitated the image of Downtown as a modern business center.

For the plaza, Isamu Noguchi created a serene sunken garden and fountain utilizing seven naturally-formed blocks of basalt from Japan's Uji River (the fountain runs only during the week). The garden can be viewed from above, and to different effect, through the windows of the branch bank in the base of the building.
On the plaza is Jean Dubuffet's Group of Four Trees (1972). The cleared space also provides a spectacular view of the towers of earlier skyscrapers that contrast so dramatically with Chase's building. To the south is the Manhattan Company Building (WS9); to the southeast is the Bank of New York (WS11); and to the east rises the Cities Service Building (NW15).

NW13 Wallace Building

56 Pine Street (Oswald Wirz, 1893-94). Speculative office building construction expanded in the final decade of the 19th century, with many buildings erected in the traditional styles favored by New York's architects and builders. James G. Wallace erected this building in what was at the time the heart of the city's insurance district: note the two buildings to the left — the Caledonian Insurance Company Building (James B. Baker, 1901-02) at Nos. 50-52 and the Sun Life Insurance Company Building (Arthur D. Pickering, 1889-90) at No. 54, with its terra-cotta sun panels. The Wallace Building, one of the hidden delights of Lower Manhattan, is a magnificent Romanesque Revival style structure faced with a beautiful reddish sandstone on the lower stories and yellow brick with matching terra-cotta trim above. The heavy round arches on the base and the superb Byzantine-style carving typify Romanesque Revival design. Note the stylized intertwining vines; the monster, fish, and human heads around the arches; the address numbers carved above the entrance arch; the twisted dwarf columns on the second story; the whimsical grimacing faces above the third story; and the terra-cotta panels on the upper floors.

Leave the plaza at the south side and turn left onto Pine Street; cross Nassau Street and continue along Pine Street.

NW14 Down Town Association

60 Pine Street (Charles Haight, 1886-87; addition, Warren & Wetmore, 1910-11). One consequence of the increasing separation of New York's business and residential districts was that businessmen could no longer easily return home for lunch. As a result, restaurants and luncheon clubs were established in Lower Manhattan. The Down Town Association is the city's oldest private luncheon club. The club had a rocky start, since its incorporation in 1860 coincided with the beginning of the Civil War. Unable to attract enough members to be viable, the club suspended operations in 1862. A group of businessmen revived the Association in 1877, and in a year's time the club had rented quarters on Pine Street and admitted 354 members. By the turn of the 20th century, membership had grown to

1,000. Membership in the Down Town Association offered many benefits beyond a midday meal: a comfortable place to transact business, a network of social and business connections, and prestige. Befitting its locality, the Down Town Association attracted mostly bankers, brokers, and lawyers. Women have been permitted to join since 1985. According to a critic writing in 1887, the club's new building was "a big house, ornate outside and sumptuous within, of which practically the sole function is to enable some hundreds of busy men to take one hurried meal a day, six days in the week, under circumstances of more exclusiveness than can be had in the restaurants." The original Romanesque Revival style brownstone, buff-colored brick, and terracotta building, designed by club member Charles Haight, was expanded to the east in 1910-11.

NW15 Cities Service Building (60 Wall Tower)
Now AIG Building, 70 Pine Street (Clinton & Russell and Holton & George, 1929-32). When this extraordinary Art Deco tower was completed, it was the tallest building in Lower Manhattan and the third tallest in the world. The building was constructed by Henry L. Doherty, industrialist, banker, major real estate investor in New York and Florida, and the founder and president of the Cities Service Oil Company. The company was formed in 1910 and soon became one of the largest public utility holding companies in the United States. When this building opened in 1932, Cities Service had assets of $1.2 billion and controlled more than two hundred electric, gas, and oil companies in 33 states stretching from Danbury, Connecticut, to Spokane, Washington. The tower on Pine Street was originally attached, via a sky bridge, to a small structure at 60 Wall Street (demolished), thus providing a prestigious Wall Street address.

Alfred Holton, chief designer of the building, created a dramatically massed structure culminating in a soaring, complexly-shaped tower, rising, as the zoning allowed, on 25 percent of the lot. The tower is capped by a crystalline glass pavilion and metal spire. The orna-

The crown of
the Cities Service
Building, c. 1932.

ment on the lower stories is quite creative, including
pairs of butterflies feeding on stylized flowers and a
huge stone model of the building above the entrance
doors to the east. Cities Service's logo, a triangle set
within a trefoil, is used as ornament on the exterior
and, most notably, around the elevator indicator lights
in the spectacular lobby. The building was the first in
the world to experiment with double-decker elevators,
which discharged passengers on two floors simultaneously. The stacked elevators could be entered at the same
time by passengers on both levels of the two-story
lobby. Although not a great success these elevators were
an interesting experiment in efficiently moving large
numbers of people without taking up excessive rental
space with elevator shafts. The elevators were

operated by "thirty young women...carefully selected and trained, with emphasis on courtesy, neatness and personality." Since the building was completed at the height of the Depression, it was important to offer potential tenants amenities that would attract them to lease space here rather than in another building. A large staff was hired to maintain the building in prime condition since, as the building manager noted, "keeping the rentable area in excellent condition is tantamount to keeping Sixty Wall Tower profitably rented." A large law library was provided to tenants (over half were lawyers), a medical clinic was available for emergencies, and meetings could be held in a furnished conference room.

The building is now the headquarters of American International Group (AIG), a global insurance company with operations in 130 countries. Founded in Shanghai in 1919 by an American entrepreneur, C. V. Starr, it offered fire and marine coverage for American insurance companies. It was the first company to sell life insurance to the Chinese people, and in ten years had offices across China and along the Pacific rim. The company opened its first office on American soil in New York City in 1926, and during succeeding decades it expanded into South America, the Middle East, Africa, and Eastern Europe.

NW16 Wall Street Plaza

88 Pine Street, at Water Street and Maiden Lane (I.M. Pei & Partners, 1968-73; James I. Freed, architect-in-charge). This minimalist building with its white steel framework and its large expanses of glass is unquestionably one of the most elegant buildings erected during the building boom of the late 1960s and early 1970s, a time when many of the exceedingly mediocre office towers on surroundings sites were rising. The balance between the rectangular window openings and the beams with their recessed rectangular panels is carefully studied. Each of the 28-foot-wide openings is filled with three sheets of glass that abut one another, creating a wonderful sense of lightness.

Walk through and admire the lobby of 70 Pine Street. Exit on Cedar Street and turn right. Turn left on Pearl Street and then right on Maiden Lane. Walk to Water Street. If the lobby is closed, continue along Pine Street and turn left on Pearl Street, walk to Maiden Lane and turn right, stopping at Water Street.

Continue along Maiden Lane to Front Street. Turn left.

NW17 Belgian Block Street Paving

Front Street is paved with stone blocks often mistakenly referred to as cobblestones, but actually known as Belgian blocks. Cobblestones, small rocks smoothed by water, were prevalent on the city's streets beginning in 1684, when present-day Stone Street was paved with them. In 1852, Fulton Street become the first thoroughfare paved with blocks of granite quarried in New England. Apparently, the blocks became known as Belgian blocks because they resemble the paving employed on Belgian streets and squares. The run of blocks along Front Street is largely intact, just waiting for the return of the metal-wheeled carts that once clattered over their uneven surfaces.

Continue along Front Street and turn right on John Street.

NW18 Hickson W. Field Stores

170-176 John Street (1840). In 1835 commission merchant Hickson Field purchased three buildings on this site and five years later replaced them with what is now the only surviving all-granite warehouse in New York City. Granite was popular for the Greek Revival warehouses erected in the seaport cities of New England, but the expense of shipping the stone to New York was prohibitive, and on most contemporary warehouses the use of granite was limited to the ground floor (see NW22). On Field's building, the granite facade is pierced by crisply cut windows and is supported on heavy granite piers. The top story is an addition from 1981-82.

NW19 A. A. Low & Brothers Stores

167-171 John Street (1850). It was a fortune made from the China trade that permitted Abiel Abbot Low to erect this impressive warehouse, as well as an enormous mansion that still stands on Pierrepont Place in Brooklyn Heights. In 1833 Low sailed to Canton, China, to work as a clerk for Russell and Company, the biggest American mercantile firm active in the China trade. He soon became a partner in the firm, but after returning to New York in 1840, he went into business for himself as A. A. Low & Brothers. The firm commanded a fleet of clipper ships — the *Houqua, Montauk, Oriental, Great Republic,* and others — whose speed outstripped the competition, making the firm a leading importer of Chinese tea and Japanese silk. At Low's death in 1893, Columbia University president Seth Low inherited his father's fortune, donating $1 million to erect Columbia's library as a memorial to his father.

The A.A. Low & Brothers Store is a rare example of a warehouse with a stone facade (the deteriorated stone is now stuccoed and painted). The cast-iron piers at the base were probably the result of an alteration in the 1860s that widened the openings, making it easier to move goods in and out of the warehouse. The building has been adapted for use as a gallery for the South Street Seaport Museum.

Retrace your steps on John Street and turn right on Front Street.

South Street Seaport Museum

In the early 1960s, Lower Manhattan's East River waterfront was still largely defined by the modest buildings erected early in the nineteenth century for the city's expanding commercial sector. A building boom in that decade wiped out most of these blocks of modest brick and granite counting-houses. In the mid-1960s a group was organized to fight for the preservation of the remaining blocks of the old seaport city, particularly those adjacent to the Fulton Fish Market. The result was the South Street Seaport Museum, which was chartered in 1967. The museum acquired several historic buildings and ships, and worked with New York State on the acquisition of Schermerhorn Row (NW21). Restoration work proceeded slowly until 1979, when the city announced that the Rouse Corporation and its architect Benjamin Thompson & Associates would restore the area as part of the creation of a "festival marketplace." The market opened in 1983 but has not been a total success. Unfortunately, the museum itself has often been lost amid the commercial development and has not attracted a large local audience. In order to increase its presence in the city, in 1998 the museum announced that a major permanent exhibition space would be created. Galleries would be located in the Low Building (NW19), on the upper floors of Schermerhorn Row, and in a strikingly modern new structure designed by Beyer Blinder Belle that will be built on the corner of John and South streets when funds are raised.

NW20 Josiah and William Macy Stores

189 Front Street (1835-36) and 191 Front Street (1860).
The brick warehouse with granite base at No. 189, a typical example of Greek Revival style commercial construction of the 1830s, was built by Nantucket ship owner
and merchant Josiah Macy. Josiah Macy became a ship-
master at a very young age, plying the trade along the
eastern seaboard and to Spain and the Mediterranean.
After the War of 1812, he moved to New York City and
began operating a New York-Liverpool packet service. In
1830 he created the shipping and commission house
Josiah Macy and Son. Following Josiah's retirement in
1853, his son William and grandson Josiah, Jr., continued the business and became increasingly involved with
the sale of sperm-whale oil, the most expensive oil used
for lighting, and then in the refining of petroleum.
Josiah, Jr. became an early supporter of John D. Rockefeller and amassed a fortune as one of the leaders of the
Standard Oil Corporation (BB11). In 1860, when the
Macys expanded their business into 191 Front Street,
they removed the late 18th-century facade of that building and erected a new front that matched their building
at No. 189, substituting modern cast iron for the granite
employed on the original storefront.

*A.A. Low & Brother's
store (center),
c.1860s. The build-
ing at the far right is
long gone and the lot
will house a new South
Street Seaport museum
building.*

Walk to Fulton
Street and turn
right.

135

Fulton Street in 1828
with Schermerhorn
Row at left and the
Fulton Market at
right.

NW21 Schermerhorn Row

2-18 Fulton Street (1810-12). Schermerhorn Row,
including the entire frontage on Fulton Street and
adjoining buildings on Front and South streets, is the
most extraordinary group of surviving early commercial
buildings in New York City. These four-story buildings,
with their handmade bricks and steep sloping roofs,
were erected on landfill in three campaigns stretching
over three construction seasons, beginning at South
Street and moving west. Wealthy merchant Peter Schermerhorn erected the row as a speculative venture (his
own counting house was at 243 Water Street), renting
out space to other merchants and entrepreneurs. At the
time of its completion, this was one of the largest urban
development projects that had ever been undertaken in
New York City. Boxes, barrels, and other goods entered
the buildings through street-level arches with brownstone surrounds, one of which survives at No. 2. Over
the years, major alterations have occurred, notably to
the storefronts, but a surprising amount of original
architectural fabric survives. The impressive mansard
roof at No. 2 was added in 1868 when the building was
converted into a hotel.

It is easy to take the presence of these buildings for
granted, but their preservation and restoration resulted
from a long battle led by the South Street Seaport

Museum. The museum and its volunteers fought the demolition of Schermerhorn Row and had the buildings designated as city landmarks in 1968. In 1974 New York State purchased the buildings, and in 1982-83 architect Jan Hird Pokorny's firm undertook the restoration and adaptation for use by the Museum and the associated marketplace (see p.134).

Retrace your steps on Fulton Street. Turn right on Water Street.

NW22 207-211 Water Street

(1835-36). These three handsomely restored counting houses typify Greek Revival commercial design of the 1830s. Each is faced with machine-made brick that is crisper than the handmade brick at Schermerhorn Row (NW21). The facades are articulated by rectangular window openings, multi-paned window sash, and simple granite sills and lintels. The boldly-scaled storefronts of New England granite are the most impressive feature, with their austere posts and horizontal lintels supporting the weight of the upper facade. Note the surviving granite rain basins. Today the storefront of No. 211 is the home of Bowne & Company, a shop and museum of printing history. One of the oldest businesses in continuous operation in New York City, Bowne & Co. was founded in 1775 by Robert Bowne as a purveyor of stationery, dry goods, and other merchandise. By the early 1800s its business had focused on commercial printing. Today the company is a leading full-service financial printer, headquartered at 345 Hudson Street.

NW23 A.A. Thompson & Co.

213-215 Water Street (Stephen Decatur Hatch, 1868). By the mid-19th century, merchants had largely abandoned the South Street Seaport area and a wide variety of marine, industrial, and storage firms moved into old buildings or erected new structures. This Italianate style building was erected by A.A. Thompson & Co., dealer in tin and other metals. The street front has a cast-iron base, but the remainder of the building is Tuckahoe marble (from Westchester County just north of New York City), the most popular material for commercial buildings in the 1850s and 1860s.

Retrace your steps on Water Street to the corner of Fulton Street

NW24 Titanic Memorial

Northeast corner Water and Fulton streets (Warren & Wetmore, 1913). On April 12, 1912, when the Titanic sank with over fifteen hundred people on board, work was just beginning on the construction of the Seamen's Church Institute's building at 25 South Street. A proposal was made that the lighthouse planned to crown this building become a memorial to those who had died in the disaster. Warren & Wetmore, architects best known for Grand Central Terminal, designed the building and the memorial, which originally included a ball that was lowered each day at the stroke of noon. When the building was demolished in 1968, the memorial was salvaged and donated to the South Street Seaport Museum.

Continue south on Water Street.

NW25 1 Seaport Plaza (Prudential Securities Building)

199 Water Street (Swanke Hayden Connell & Partners, 1982-83). In order to partially fund the restoration of Schermerhorn Row, a portion of its development rights (or air rights) was sold to the owner of this site. The scale of this massive stone skyscraper results from the purchase of these development rights, which added additional bulk to that permitted under the city's zoning code. The lobby, entered from Water Street, was designed to incorporate three large works by Frank Stella — one of America's most prominent post-war artists — dating from 1969-70. The building is the headquarters of Prudential Securities, the brokerage arm of the Prudential Insurance Company, America's biggest insurer. It began as the brokerage firm J. S. Bache & Co., whose origins date back to 1879. The Bache firm was notable for its strong branch-office system (it had 37 offices and 800 employees in 1945), which marketed securities to the middle-class investor. Expanding into a broad range of financial services, Prudential bought the Bache firm in 1981.

Continue south on Water Street. Turn right on John Street and walk to the corner of Cliff Street.

NW26 John Street Insurance District.

After banking, insurance was the earliest financial business to develop in New York City. Initially it supported the port, protecting ships and cargoes against loss; it quickly expanded into fire insurance as well. Beginning in 1843, the Mutual Life Insurance Company was the first to offer life insurance policies. In the 19th century, the insurance business centered on Wall, Pine, and Cedar streets from Broadway to William Street (NW12). As the industry grew and as insurance companies erected ever-more-spectacular buildings, the district expanded. By the 1920s insurance companies were moving north in what one commentator noted was "a great tidal wave." John Street became the center for the construction of a series of office buildings erected both by speculative investors and by individual insurance firms for their own headquarters (many are now apartments).

In order to attract insurance companies, the new buildings on John Street had to provide light-filled offices and flexible floor space that would be suitable for both small and large companies. The earliest of the major John Street buildings was the **Insurance Center Building** at 80 John Street (26a), southwest corner Gold Street (Buchman & Kahn, 1925-27). This is one of the first buildings erected in New York that shows the influence of the 1925 Exposition des Arts Decoratif et Industriel Moderne in Paris. Architect Ely Jacques Kahn had visited the exhibit and, upon his return, introduced the ornamental use of zigzag detail on the frieze above the third floor of this building. These angular zigzags, juxtaposed with organic curving petal forms, became a key decorative element of Art Deco design. Kahn's most important building in Lower Manhattan is the **Insurance Building** at 111 John Street (26b), on the northeast corner of Cliff Street (Buchman & Kahn, 1928-29), described in New York The Wonder City as "both a giant and an 'aristocrat' among the mammoth office buildings catering to insurance interests." The cliff-like setbacks are a creative adaptation of the massing required under the 1916 zoning law (see p. 125), and the brick detailing reflects Kahn's interest in adapting textile designs to building facades. At 101 John Street, on the northwest corner of Cliff Street is the limestone building erected as

Walk to Gold
Street and turn
left. Walk two
blocks to Maiden
Lane.

the New York headquarters of the **Insurance Company
of North America** (26c), America's first insurance company, founded in Philadelphia in 1792. Designed by
Shreve, Lamb & Harmon (1932-33), architect of the
Empire State Building, this was the last of the pre-World
War II office buildings begun in Lower Manhattan. It is
virtually devoid of ornament, and several critics have
noted that it introduced a new sense of Modernism to
the design of commercial skyscrapers.

*Federal Reserve Bank,
c.1935, just after the
William Street addi-
tion was completed.*

NW27 Roosevelt & Son Building

90 Maiden Lane (attributed to Charles Wright, 1870-71). Roosevelt & Son, the country's leading importers of plate glass and mirrors, expanded its premises in 1870 and remodeled two adjacent Maiden Lane warehouses by erecting an impressive cast-iron facade crowned by a French Second Empire style mansard roof. Among the partners in the Roosevelt Company in 1870 was Theodore Roosevelt, Sr., father of the future president.

NW28 Louise Nevelson Plaza

William Street, Liberty Street, and Maiden Lane (Louise Nevelson, 1977-78). As part of a project to improve traffic flow in Lower Manhattan, the buildings on this triangle were demolished, Liberty Street was widened, and the city commissioned a work from the prominent New York sculptor Louise Nevelson. Nevelson created *Shadows and Flags*, a series of seven Cor-ten steel "trees" painted black, juxtaposed with a group of real trees. This became the first space in New York City named for an artist.

NW29 Federal Reserve Bank

33 Liberty Street (York & Sawyer, 1919-24; addition, 1934-35). The Federal Reserve System is the central bank of the United States, created by Congress in 1913 to regulate the money supply, supervise banks, and maintain the stability of the nation's financial system. One of twelve district banks throughout the country, the Federal Reserve Bank of New York is the largest, busiest, and most influential. The New York Fed implements monetary policy through its "open market operations" — buying or selling Treasury securities on the secondary market to ease or constrict the amount of credit in the banking system. It also trades in the foreign exchange markets to regulate the value of the dollar according to Federal Reserve Board policy. The Fed circulates the nation's currency, serves as the banker to the United States government, and is its fiscal agent for all international financial dealings. The world's largest con-

Turn right on Maiden Lane and walk to Louise Nevelson Plaza. Notice the view of the Chase Manhattan Bank Building (NW12) and the Manhattan Company Building (WS9).

Stand on the southeast corner of Liberty and William streets.

centration of gold — bricks valued at $86 billion — is stored on behalf of foreign nations and financial institutions in the Fed's vaults five stories below street level.

In 1919 a competition was held for the design of the New York branch of the Federal Reserve, which would be the largest bank building in America. Appropriately, the competition was won by York & Sawyer, a firm that specialized in bank design, creating many of America's finest early-20th-century bank buildings. *The Real Estate Record* noted late in 1919 when the design was made public, that the building was "designed in a modified Florentine [Renaissance] style of architecture, adapted to American ideas and the peculiarities of the downtown business district." The building is clad in massive blocks

---

Samuel Yellin

At a time when banks and large corporate office buildings were embellished with lavish detail that was often intentionally added to give a new building the aura of age, architects frequently commissioned iron detail in historic styles. The greatest iron designer of the early decades of the 20th century was

Door to teller's space at Federal Reserve Bank.

Samuel Yellin. Yellin was born in Galicia (Poland) and apprenticed with a Russian ironworker. Before settling in Philadelphia in 1906, Yellin worked in Belgium and England, often reproducing ancient ironwork. Despite the artistry of his work and the recognition and many awards that he received, Yellin always referred to himself as just a "blacksmith." Yellin was at his best creating magnificent modern adaptations of medieval Gothic and Italian Renaissance forms, as is evident in the lamps that mark the main entrance to the Federal Reserve Bank. Among the buildings in New York City graced with Yellin's ironwork are three on these tours — the Federal Reserve Bank (NW29), with its exterior lamps and window guards and its extensive array of interior iron elements; the Cunard Building (BB14), with its interior gates and screens; and the entrance doors and interior fittings added by Lehman Brothers when it altered the Seligman & Company Building (WS17).

142

of rusticated stone, giving it a feeling of impregnability
and making a powerful statement about the stability of
the federal government and of the American banking
system. The initial site assemblage did not include the
William Street frontage, which was finally purchased in
1934 and filled with an addition that includes a rounded
corner tower facing Maiden Lane. The only ornamental
flourishes on the exterior are the iron window screens
and the elegant lamps at the main entrance farther east
on Liberty Street — all the work of ironmaster Samuel
Yellin. The austere, vaulted Early Renaissance-inspired
lobby and public bank on the first floor are worth visiting, especially to view Yellin's magnificent iron lamps,
screens, gates, and furnishings.

Walk west on
Liberty Street to
the corner of
Nassau Street.

NW30 Liberty Tower

55 Liberty Street, northwest corner Nassau Street
(Henry Ives Cobb, 1909-10). Employing a striking
architectural design was one stratagem that speculative
builders employed to attract attention and tenants to
their buildings. For Liberty Tower, located on a small
plot at what was, in 1909, the northern fringe of the
financial district, a group of St. Louis investors commissioned a steel-framed building clad in gleaming
white terra-cotta, with ornate Gothic detail and a
prominent roofline bristling with gables, pinnacles,
lions, and eagles. Look carefully at the whimsical terra-
cotta detail: grotesque figures peer down from the
23rd story, while alligators crawl up the entrance arch.
From 1919 to 1945 this was the headquarters of the
Sinclair Oil Company; in 1979 the building was converted into apartments.

Walk west on
Liberty Street.

NW31 Chamber of Commerce of the State of New York

Now International Commercial Bank of China, 65 Liberty Street (James B. Baker, 1900-01). New York's
Chamber of Commerce was the first mercantile association in America. Established in 1768 by twenty merchants, it promoted commerce, mediated trade disputes,
and lobbied for laws that would facilitate trade and
industry. Its earliest meetings, held at Fraunces Tavern

Chamber of Commerce Building, c.1901.

(BB29), were a mixture of business and pleasure: the Chamber's rules directed the treasurer to provide "Bread and Cheese, Beer, Punch, Pipes and Tobacco" for its members' enjoyment. The Revolutionary War divided the Chamber's membership, and its Loyalist faction remained in the city during the British occupation. In 1784, after the war's end, the Chamber was reorganized with a new charter as a thoroughly patriotic American institution. The Chamber of Commerce promoted numerous important commercial improvements: in 1786 it lent its support to development of the Erie Canal; it was a backer of the transatlantic cable; several of its members served on the Rapid Transit Commission which developed New York City's subway system; and it encouraged the construction of the Catskill aqueduct in 1912. The Chamber was also responsible for several public monuments, proposing and raising funds for the George Washington statue at Federal Hall (WS5) and the

144

statue of General William Tecumseh Sherman at Grand Army Plaza. In 1980 the Chamber moved out of this building, and in 1996 it merged with the New York City Partnership, a civic and business organization.

The design of this dynamic Beaux-Arts style structure centers on the Great Hall, a richly ornamented room with walls that were covered in member's portraits. The street facades, clad in white Vermont marble capped by an elaborate mansard roof, were once embellished with three sculpture groups by Daniel Chester French; these deteriorated and were removed. A Taiwanese bank has adapted the Great Hall for modern banking needs.

Return to Nassau Street and turn left; walk to Maiden Lane.

NW32 2 Federal Reserve Plaza
33 Maiden Lane (Phillip Johnson/John Burgee, 1980-85). This is one of a series of Postmodern buildings designed by Philip Johnson's firm in the 1970s and 1980s that borrowed forms from historical buildings. The mock-medieval detail, which adapts the tower motif from the nearby Federal Reserve Bank (NW29), has a particularly flimsy look, especially when compared to the design of its masterful neighbor.

Cross Maiden Lane and Nassau Street and continue north a few yards on Nassau Street.

NW33 63 Nassau Street
(attributed to James Bogardus, c. 1860). The design of this modest cast-iron building has been attributed to James Bogardus, the first person to use cast iron for building facades. The structure was once ornamented with portrait busts of George Washington and Benjamin Franklin (only the Franklin busts are extant), a favorite decorative device employed by Bogardus.

Continue up Nassau Street and turn right on John Street.

NW34 John Street United Methodist Church
44 John Street (attributed to William Hurry, 1841). John Street is the oldest Methodist church organization in the United States, established by Philip Embury and Barbara Heck in 1766. It has occupied this site since 1768. The present brownstone-fronted building, combining features of Federal, Greek Revival, and Italianate design, is the third church on the site. When John Street was widened in 1836, the society debated whether to

John Street Methodist Church flanked by 1830s counting-houses, c.1887.

rebuild or move to a residential neighborhood closer to its congregants. The importance of the site in the history of Methodism prompted the members to erect a smaller building on John Street, incorporating salvaged roof timbers and fixtures from the previous church. Among the early members of the congregation was Peter Williams, a slave who served as church sexton and who, after gaining his freedom, founded the African Methodist Episcopal (A.M.E.) denomination.

"What shall I say of a city that builds the most beautiful cathedral in the world and calls it an office building?"
—British Prime Minister Arthur Balfour

One of America's earliest and greatest romantic skyscrapers, rising 60 stories over City Hall Park, the Woolworth Building held the coveted title of world's tallest building from 1913 until losing it in 1929 to the Chrysler Building. The Gothic-inspired, terra-cotta clad skyscraper was built — and paid for in cash — by the inventor of that great American institution , the five and ten cent store. When asked why he did it, Frank Woolworth said he wanted the building to advertise his stores. There's also a story about his competition with the Metropolitan Life Insurance Company, which refused Woolworth a mortgage and then watched its own famous tower relegated to second-tallest status.

Wander into what was once called the "Cathedral of Commerce," and you will find yourself in an arcade resplendent in marble walls, bronze Gothic filigree, and golden mosaics. Mimicking the nave and transept plan of church architecture, the Woolworth's lobby rises to a gleaming vaulted ceiling. Voluptuous Gothic detail ranges from elaborately finished mailboxes to altarpieces of "Labor" and "Commerce" on the mezzanines. Sculpted caricatures by Tom Johnson show architect Cass Gilbert holding a model of the building, Frank Woolworth counting his nickels and dimes, the builder, and the structural engineer. Even the rental agent, Edward J. Hogan, was depicted in a gargoyle, but only after he protested in a letter to Gilbert that he was being left out.

Heritage Trails Site Marker #R4: 233 Broadway, between Barclay Street and Park Place

Newspaper Row

Back in the era before radio, television, or the Internet, when the newspaper was the principal medium of communication, the tall building along Park Row former "newspaper row" in the larger "printing house square'" the great district of the city's — and the nation's — newspaper trade. Here Joseph Pulitzer presided over *The World* in the gilded dome of the Pulitzer Building, hoping to scoop his neighbors, the *New York Times*, the *Tribune*, and the *Sun*. On nearby streets, the *Evening Journal*, the *Evening Post*, the *Herald*, the *Mail* and the *Express* competed — back when New York supported some 20 English-language daily papers, not to mention the weeklies and countless foreign-language sheets.

Convenient to both Wall Street and City Hall, they printed the stories of business and politics. By the turn of the century, however, as businesses began to move uptown, the papers followed. The *Herald* moved to Sixth Avenue and 34th street (which became Herald Square) and the *Times* to Broadway and 42nd Street (Times Square). By the 1930's, newspaper row was empty. Today's papers, far fewer in number, are published all around town.

Heritage Trails Site Marker #R9: In City Hall Park, near corner of Park Row and Spruce Street

148

The elegant Anglo-French splendor of City Hall survives from a time when classical grace was a civic ideal, New York City government could fit into one small building, and this part of Downtown was still Uptown. The building opened in 1812 and has served ever since as the seat of municipal governance of New York. The competition winning design was by Joseph Francois Mangin, a Frenchman, and John J. McComb, Jr., a Scot.

Today, City Hall takes center stage in as the ceremonial heart of our nation's major metropolitan civic center. Within its marble walls, Mayors hold court, the City Council holds forth, and the press and public are invited to witness the splendid, if chaotic, spectacle of municipal democracy in action.

City Hall Park is twice as old as City Hall, part of a large tract reserved by the Dutch colonists as New Amsterdam's commons. From as early as the 1730's, the park has served as New York's official public square, backdrop to centuries of celebration and mourning. Recent renovations have left it looking better than ever.

Heritage Trails Site Marker #R5: In northern part of park opposite front steps of City Hall

Though old city maps show an African Burial Ground near Broadway and Chambers Street, it was not until 1991 that anyone realized thousands of burials still existed twenty feet below sea level. Further investigation confirmed that this was one of New York City's major Colonial-era sites; an African burial ground dating back to the 18th and possibly even the 17th century, one of very few surviving anywhere in the Americas, and now the largest known excavated African cemetery in the world.

The African Burial Ground was active until 1794. Within an area of not quite six acres, perhaps as many as 20,000 people were interred, mostly free or enslaved Africans. During the 18th century, one in ten residents of New York were of African descent, and slavery was widespread in and near the city. The institution of slavery officially ended in New York on July 4th, 1827 — a fact celebrated by a parade through the city of hundreds of African-Americans. However, enslaved persons were in fact held in New York beyond that date.

Heritage Trails Site Marker #R6: At Duane and Elk Streets, nearby to Foley Square/Civic Center

The burials were discovered by archaeologists digging in advance of the construction of a new federal building. When bulldozers moved in, angry protests and congressional hearings led to an Act of Congress that stopped the destruction. But beforehand, over 400 burials were disinterred. Now designated officially as a city, state, and federal landmark, the African Burial Ground testifies to the centuries-old history of African-Americans in New York.

Local Resources

For additional information about Lower Manhattan and activities in New York City's downtown, contact the following organizations:

Alliance for Downtown New York, Inc.
120 Broadway, Suite 3340, New York, N.Y. 10271
212-566-6700 www.DowntownNY.com

Conservancy for Historic Battery Park
120 Broadway, Suite 3340, New York, N.Y. 10271
212-835-2750 www.thebattery.org

Heritage Trails New York
c/o Alliance for Downtown New York, Inc.
   (see above)
www.heritagetrails.org

Museum of American Financial History
26 Broadway, New York, NY 10004
212-908-4519 www.mafh.org

National Park Service
Federal Hall National Monument
26 Wall Street, New York, N.Y. 10005
212-825-6888 www.nps.gov

The Skyscraper Museum
212-968-1961 www.skyscraper.org

South Street Seaport Museum
207 Front Street, New York, N.Y. 10038
212-748-8600 www.southstseaport.org

World Financial Center
Winter Garden at Battery Park City
West Street, between Liberty and Vesey Streets
212-945-0505 www.worldfinancialcenter.com

Selected Bibliography

Buck, James E., ed., *The New York Stock Exchange: The First 200 Years.* Essex, Ct: Greenwich Publishing Group, 1992.

Carosso, Vincent P. *Investment Banking in America: A History.* Cambridge: Harvard University Press, 1970.

Dolkart, Andrew S., *Forging a Metropolis: Walking Tours of Lower Manhattan Architecture.* NY: Whitney Museum of American Art, 1990.

Dolkart, Andrew S., *Guide to New York City Landmarks.* NY: New York City Landmarks Preservation Commission and John Wiley & Sons, 1998.

Geisst, Charles R., *Wall Street: A History.* NY: Oxford University Press, 1997.

Landau, Sarah Bradford and Carl W. Condit, *Rise of the New York Skyscraper 1865-1913.* New Haven: Yale University Press, 1996.

Myers, Margaret G. *A Financial History of the United States.* NY: Columbia University Press, 1970.

Severini, Lois, *The Architecture of Finance: Early Wall Street.* Ann Arbor: UMI Research Press, 1983.

Stern, Robert, Thomas Mellins and David Fishman, *New York 1880: Architecture and Urbanism in the Gilded Age.* NY: Monacelli, 1999.

Stern, Robert A.M., Gregory Gilmartin, and John Massengale, *New York 1900: Metropolitan Architecture and Urbanism 1890-1915.* NY: Rizzoli, 1983.

Stern, Robert A.M., Gregory Gilmartin, and Thomas Mellins, *New York 1930: Architecture and Urbanism Between the Two World Wars.* NY: Rizzoli, 1987.

Stern, Robert A.M., Thomas Mellins, and David Fishman, *New York 1960: Architecture and Urbanism Between the Second World War and the Bicentennial.* NY: Monacelli, 1995.

Werner, Walter and Steven T. Smith, *Wall Street.* NY: Columbia University Press, 1991.

Willis Carol, *Form Follows Finance: Skyscrapers and Skylines in New York and Chicago.* NY: Princeton Architectural Press, 1995.

Illustration Sources

Archives and Libraries

Avery Architectural and Fine Arts Library, Drawings and Archives Department, Columbia University in the City of New York: p. 16

Bank of New York: p. 32

Beyer Blinder Belle Architects & Planners, LLP: p. 134

Chase Manhattan Archives: pp. 26, 126

Corbis/Bettman - Gendreau: p. 62
Corbis/Bettman - Underhill: pp. 123, 125, 140
Corbis/Underwood & Underwood: p. 102

Heritage Trails New York: pp. 110, 147, 148, 149, 150

J. Koehler, NY: p. 63

Landmark Society of Western New York: p. 24

R. Lorenz: pp. 76, 77, 78, 79, 108, 109, 111

Museum of the City of New York: Frontispiece, pp. 4, 13, 49, 50, 51, 52, 54, 61, 68, 90, 95, 98, 131, 135

The New-York Historical Society: pp. 15, 19, 20, 56, 117, 121, 136, 146

New York Public Library: pp. 70, 73, 80, 92, 106, 114

New York Stock Exchange Archives: Cover, pp. 29, 34, 37, 39, 42, 64, 85, 86, 89, 91, 97, 144

Publications

The Architect Magazine: p. 96 (March 1929)

Architecture and Builder Magazine: p. 58 (August 1921)

Architectural Forum Magazine: p. 118 (June 1935)

Architecture: pp. 65 (October 1929), 142 (May 1927)

Ralph Walker, Architect, pub. Henahan House, New York, 1957: p. 28

Royal Institute of British Architects Journal: p. 74 (March 14, 1912)

Index to Tours

Note: specific building addresses are listed as sub-entries under the street name where the building is located.

Page numbers in italics refer to captions, illustrations and sidebars.

National City Bank, 97-98, 98, 103
National Museum of the American Indian, 50
National Park Service, 76
Netherlands Memorial Flagpole, 46
Nevelson, Louise, 141
New Amsterdam
    Castello Plan and, 13, 14
    colonial demographics, 12-13
    Dutch colonization of, 12-14
    historic street plan, 51
    See also New York
New Deal, 40-41
New Jersey, 48
Newspaper Row, 150
New York
    British colonization of, 14
    development as banking center, 32-33
    downtown economic output, 30
    geography and economy of, 31
    historic street plan, 51
    as hub for shipping, 31, 41
    insurance industry development in, 33-34
    as leader in architecture, 16
    merger with Brooklyn, 110
    mid-nineteenth century sanitation conditions, 17-18
    post-colonial population growth, 14
    skyline, 24-25
    view in 1850 of, 29
    water shortage in, 94
    zoning regulation in, 23, 24, 25-26, 125
New York Central Railroad, 37
New York City Landmarks Preservation Commission, 71
New York City Partnership, 145
New York Cotton Exchange Building (60 Beaver Street), 103
New York Information Technology Center (55 Broad Street), 108
New York Insurance Company, 15, 16, 33
New York Landmarks Conservancy, 10
    founding and initial focus of, 9
New York Life Insurance and Trust Company, 33
New York Mirror, 16
New-York Prices Current, The, 31
New York Sports Club (30 Wall Street) (formerly U.S. Assay Office), 93
New York Stock and Exchange Board, 35
New York Stock Exchange (8-18 Broad Street), 12, 23, 34, 85, 90-91, 91, 94, 99
    crash of 1929, 40
    formation of, 35
    during Great Depression, 41

new trading facility of, 43
    1987 crash, 42
    railroad stocks and bonds, 36
    women traders on, 40, 42
    See also Bonds; Investment banking; Stocks
New York The Wonder City (Chase), 93, 101, 139
New York Unearthed (17 State Street), 78
Noguchi, Isamu, 119, 126, 128

Old Slip, 100 Old Slip (First Precinct Police Station), 107

Pacific Insurance Company, 33
Palmedo, Lillian Gaertner, 70
Panic of 1873, 19
Park Avenue, 30
Pearl Street, 19
    54 Pearl Street (Fraunces Tavern), 9, 72-74, 73
    Tappan Store on, 16, 16
    Vietnam Veterans Memorial, 74, 79
Pei, I.M., 26, 132
Phenix Bank, 16
Pickering, Arthur D., 129
Pickford, Mary, 38
Pier A (in Battery Park), 48, 49
Pierce, Melusina Fay, 73
Pine Street, 17
    54 Pine Street (Sun Life Insurance Building), 129
    56 Pine Street (Wallace Building), 21, 129
    60 Pine Street (Down Town Association), 129-30
    70 Pine Street (Cities Service Building), 23, 24, 24, 26, 130-32
    88 Pine Street (Wall Street Plaza), 26, 132
Plazas, skyscrapers and, 25-26
Pokorny, Jan Hird, 137
Population growth, post-colonial, 14
Post, George B., 90
Price, Bruce, 122, 124
Prime, Ward & King (investment bank), 36
Prudential Securities, 27
Prudential Securities Building (199 Water Street/1 Seaport Plaza), 138
Puerto Rico Telephone Company, 69
Pulitzer, Joseph, 150
Putnam's Magazine, 17

Queen Elizabeth (ship), 57
Queen Mary (ship), 57
Queens Head Tavern, 73
Queen Street (now Pearl Street), 73